COLUMBIA GLOBAL REPORTS

Dear Reader,

In early 2020, Columbia Global Reports published *Vigil*, by the East Asian historian Jeffrey Wasserstrom, which predicted the crackdown on protest and civil liberties that the government of Hong Kong initiated a few weeks later. Wasserstrom's prescience and expertise drew a good deal of positive attention to the book.

With *The Milk Tea Alliance*, Wasserstrom returns to look at where protest in East Asia is going now. The title refers to a loose companionship between pro-democracy activists in three countries where people prefer to drink their tea mixed with dairy products—unlike people in the region's dominant power, China, who traditionally don't mix their tea with anything. Through many years of deep engagement in the region, Wasserstrom has earned a rare degree of trust from these activists. This enables him to give us intimate pictures of the lives and activities of significant rising leaders who are not familiar to American readers: Netiwit Chotiphatphaisal, in Thailand, Agnes Chow, in Hong Kong, and Ye Myint Win (known as Nickey Diamond), now living in exile from Burma. He also sketches out more broadly the situations of the democracy movements in Thailand, Hong Kong, and Burma.

The days when people were predicting that China and its neighbors would naturally move toward democracy now seem like ancient history, but *The Milk Tea Alliance* is a profoundly optimistic book. By vividly showing us the courage and determination of his main characters, and their ability to attract a following, especially in the rising generation, he leaves us hopeful that the region's slide toward authoritarianism can be halted or reversed, and that a better future is possible.

Best,

Nicholas Lemann

Y0-ASU-049

COLUMBIA GLOBAL REPORTS
NEW YORK

The Milk Tea Alliance
Inside Asia's Struggle Against Autocracy and Beijing

Jeffrey Wasserstrom
With contributions by
Prad Sirisomboon*

*A pseudonym

The Milk Tea Alliance:
Inside Asia's Struggle Against Autocracy and Beijing
Copyright © 2025 by Jeffrey Wasserstrom
All rights reserved

Published by Columbia Global Reports
91 Claremont Avenue, Suite 515
New York, NY 10027
globalreports.columbia.edu

Library of Congress Cataloging-in-Publication Data
TK

Book design by Kelly Winton
Map design by Jeffrey L. Ward
Author photograph by Audrey Fong

Printed in the United States of America

To Miklós Haraszti (of Hungary's 1968 generation) and Tun Myint (of Burma's 1988 generation). Each has taught me much over the years about the value of friendships that cross borders, and about what hoping against hope means—and why it matters.

CONTENTS

Introduction

Part One
Thailand

Part Two
Hong Kong

Part Three
Burma

Conclusion—Beginnings

Further Reading

Acknowledgments

Notes

Introduction

When future historians settle down to pore over the documents, records, and artifacts of the 1960s, it seems likely that they will refer to this era as a decade of student dissent.... The dissent of youth in the 1960s was not confined to geographical regions, economic zones, or ideological spheres....
—Edward Beauchamp, 1970

It is too soon to tell if historians of the future will see the ten-year period that began in 2014 and is ending in 2024 as I finish this book the way many now see the 1960s: as a period defined by a dizzyingly wide array of struggles in which young people played central roles. This is, though, a very real possibility.

The year 2014 saw multiple protests that bear similarities with the '60s, including the Hong Kong Umbrella Movement that made Joshua Wong internationally famous while still in his teens, and the Sunflower Movement in Taiwan that pushed back against Chinese influence. In Bangkok, there were small but daring student protests against Prayuth Chan-ocha, who as Commander-in-Chief of the Royal Thai Army led a coup d'état that May that replaced the democratically elected government of Yingluck Shinawatra with a junta.

Early in 2024, a wave of pro-Palestinian demonstrations, the biggest surge of American campus activism in decades, took place. In between came the environmental protests that made a very young Greta Thunberg a global icon, as well as hundreds of Black Lives Matter marches involving mostly people in their teens and early twenties. Two peak years for youth activism were 2019 and 2020, when young people protested everywhere from Minneapolis to Minsk and from Beirut to Bogota.

Hong Kong was the site of massive protests in 2019, after the government introduced a bill that would allow China to arrest and extradite prisoners to the mainland, including political enemies. More than a million protesters took to the streets, and pro-democracy parties won a landslide in a local election in November. But exhaustion, arrests, intimidation, endless tear gas volleys by the police, and finally the outbreak of COVID stalled the movement's momentum. By the summer Beijing imposed a national security law and scuttled new elections. More than a hundred opposition figures have since been arrested in the crackdown and the most influential leading independent media outlets have been closed, their publishers persecuted under the terms of old British colonial sedition laws in some cases, the new National Security Law in others.

Some of the most dramatic demonstrations in 2020 took place in Bangkok, as university students led massive protests calling for Prayuth to resign and criticizing the Thai monarchy that had helped him stay in power, after the regime dissolved the progressive Future Forward Party. It was the biggest Thai student movement of this century. It laid the groundwork for the Move Forward Party, successor to the Future Forward Party, to win the most votes of any organization in a 2023 national election, with some former student leaders gaining seats in parliament. Then, in a replay of the past, the establishment elite succeeded in thwarting the popular will and dissolved the party.

In Burma,* the early 2020s were even more intense—and took the darkest turn of all. After the party of State Counselor Aung San Suu Kyi won a general election in a landslide, before the new parliament members could even be sworn in, the military staged a coup. The military had retained its hold on many institutions even during the apparent democratization of the 2010s during which it released Suu Kyi from house arrest and allowed her party some say in government. It has now regained control of all levers of power and taken Suu Kyi into custody.

A wave of protests, dubbed the Spring Revolution, erupted. For a time, with crowds filling the streets and anti-coup chants and songs filling the air, there was a triumphant air in Burma. It seemed that a miraculous People Power moment might be on the horizon.

In Burma, as in Thailand, the early 2020s have seen events that trigger a sense of déjà vu. The aftermath of the initial, hopeful days of the Spring Revolution—originally a non-violent movement that has turned violent—called to mind the events of 1988. That year saw a People Power–like uprising that nearly ended decades of military rule before being brutally suppressed. Shortly after, Aung San Suu Kyi began the first of her multiple periods under house arrest. The Spring Revolution's first phase was similarly curtailed with brute force as troops opened fire on protesters in the streets of Yangon. In response, the opposition formed armed wings, some of them described as being part of a "People's Defense Force," which joined the civil war against the junta that was already being fought by long-established groups in some areas. New independent armed groups also emerged

---

*The country is known as both Burma and Myanmar. I will use Burma here, as it is more familiar to general readers and was commonly used in the past.

to try to end military rule, echoing past events like 1988, when peaceful protests were similarly met with violence.

Burma's latest crackdowns and civil wars have taken a devastating toll. Since early 2021, state violence and skirmishes have reportedly caused between 5,000 and 6,000 deaths, with 3 million people internally displaced. These figures, however, don't account for those who have died from neglect under the junta's misrule or from the collapse of the healthcare system, which war has hollowed out, making it nearly impossible to respond effectively to natural disasters and humanitarian crises.

The political situations in Burma, Thailand, and Hong Kong are radically different. Only Burma is in a state of civil war.* Only Hong Kong has changed in just a few years from a place with virtually no political prisoners to one with many. Only Thailand has lèse-majesté laws that criminalize any criticism of the monarchy. And yet, many young pro-democracy activists in and exiles from these three places routinely refer to a sense that their struggles are related.

They adopt tactics from one another and share tools and songs. Umbrellas were iconic in the 2014 and 2019 Hong Kong protests and later became central to demonstrations in Bangkok in 2020. In 2021, Burmese protesters banged pots during the anti-coup movement, a practice later taken up by some Bangkok demonstrators. Similarly, protest songs sung in Thai on one side of the Thailand-Burma border began to be sung in Burmese on the other. The activists express solidarity both online and in the streets, sharing information and resources. Young activists

* At present, fighting is taking place across the country, but some regions have experienced nearly continuous conflict for decades between insurgent groups seeking independence and government forces.

in Hong Kong even created a crowdsourced Google document, summarizing lessons they had learned from their 2019 movement, which was translated into Burmese, so that it could be read by anti-coup activists in Burma.

People living in or exiled from these regions feel that their struggles—despite slim chances of short-term success—share important characteristics. This book explores the sense of connection across geographical, cultural, and linguistic divides, often referred to as the "Milk Tea Alliance." Coined in early 2020, the term highlights the popularity of dairy-based tea drinks in many parts of Asia but not mainland China, where tea has traditionally been consumed without dairy.*

Netizens in Hong Kong, Bangkok, and Taipei joined together as a bloc in April 2020 to push back against jingoistic mainland supporters of the Chinese Communist Party. The term "Milk Tea Alliance" took off as a transnational symbol of resistance against Beijing's influence. Memes soon appeared across the web featuring cups of Hong Kong milk tea, Thai tea with condensed milk, and Taiwan's bubble tea with tapioca.

This online movement was part of a larger trend rooted in personal connections forged during the mid-2010s and expanding significantly by 2019 and the 2020s. Struggles across Asia's Pacific Rim became increasingly interconnected as participants displayed greater solidarity and exchanged tactics. Examples include a Thai activist singing a banned Hong Kong song in Bangkok in October 2020, Hong Kong protesters

---

*The Milk Tea Alliance is a flexible entity that connects movements across Asia, including India, Indonesia, Taiwan, Tibet, Hong Kong, Thailand, and Burma. This discussion focuses on Hong Kong, Thailand, and Burma, with nods to Taiwan and Tibet. While it is difficult to pinpoint its origin, the phrase "Milk Tea Alliance" gained prominence in April 2020.

gathering outside the Thai consulate around the same time to condemn police violence in Thailand, and Thai activists joining Burmese locals in Bangkok in early 2021 to protest the recent coup in Burma.

Linkages have taken various forms. In mid-2021, the Burmese hip-hop group Rap Against Junta led the creation of a video titled "Dictators Must Die," featuring rappers from across Asia, including Hong Kong, delivering rhymed critiques of autocrats. The video shows images of protests and state violence involving leaders like Xi Jinping and Southeast Asian generals. The Burmese group drew inspiration from the Thai band Rap Against Dictatorship, one of whose members contributed lyrics to the collective number expressing the generational anger driving many protests:

> Get retired you old men,
> It's time for the new gen.
> Watch now, the game is on,
> Dictators, move along.

While dictators still hold power in many regions, hope persists within segments of the Milk Tea Alliance, even though victories are rare and opponents are better funded and armed. History shows that hope has endured in similarly bleak circumstances, such as South Africa under apartheid, Taiwan under martial law, and Czechoslovakia after the Prague Spring. Many Milk Tea Alliance activists find inspiration in writings by Václav Havel and quotes from Nelson Mandela, symbols of resilience against oppressive regimes.

Young activists have been drawing on similar pop culture symbols, with rap as just one example. In several Asian regions, they donned Guy Fawkes masks, sang "Do You Hear the People Sing?" from *Les Misérables*, and found inspiration in stories of young people battling powerful forces in a David-versus-Goliath fashion. The *Harry Potter* series also influenced some activists in the region.

The *Hunger Games* novels and the movies based on them had even more impact. This popular culture text may have roots in the West, but its inspirational power has been greatest in Asia. The impact of this mythic tale on youths has shown through via variations in local languages of one of its slogans: "If we burn, you burn with us." It has shown through even more in the use of the three-finger salute of defiance that *Hunger Games* hero Katniss Everdeen deploys, borrowing it, tellingly, from a nearby homeland that like hers is oppressed by a common capital, doing so to honor an ally from that other place who has died.

First used in 2014 and 2015, when youths in Hong Kong, Thailand, and Burma occasionally flashed it, the three-finger salute became a powerful gesture in Bangkok during the early 2020s, with nearly every major activist and progressive political candidate photographed using it. Its most significant impact has been in Burma, where it is now ubiquitous in the resistance struggle. The salute features prominently in street protests, in Rap Against Junta videos, and was notably displayed by the Burmese representative to the UN during a speech asserting his opposition to the junta, symbolizing solidarity with his homeland's counterparts to Katniss and her fellow resistance fighters.

The two figures I will focus on from here are a Hong Kong activist and a Thai activist: Agnes Chow and Netiwit

Chotiphatphaisal. My aim in highlighting them is not to use their biographies or their networks to provide an overview of the Milk Tea Alliance or the Hong Kong and Thai democracy movements. I do not consider them the most important leaders in these movements, nor do I suggest that their generation is the only one that matters. Rather, I am interested in using the stories of Chow, Netiwit,* and other remarkable young people engaged in underdog struggles in Asia to explore themes of motivation, persistence, and resilience.

A third activist, Burma's Ye Myint Win—known internationally as Nickey Diamond[†]—will also be discussed. Though a dozen years older than Chow and Netiwit, Diamond, like them, began his activism in the early 2010s. To contextualize his story, I will introduce the experiences of my longtime friend Tun Myint,[‡] an older Burmese activist who began his struggle in 1988. By moving across settings and, in Burma's case, across generations, I hope to show connections between these three movements, despite their distinct histories.

Thinking about Chow, Netiwit, and Diamond as a trio (though the first two will get much more attention), readers should realize they make up a varied group—and not just because they come from places that, due to a mix of linguistic and other

---

*In Thai, it is the convention to refer to people after first mention by their first names.

[†] "Nickey Diamond" may sound like a name invented by a novelist, but it is not. Foreign friends gave him the English first name when he was around twenty, and "Diamond" is the English translation of part of his father's name.

[‡] Tun Myint is a common name in Burma. The Tun Myint in this book is not the one who served as an elected official, nor the one who acted as an informant for the junta.

issues, were rarely grouped together by analysts before the Milk Tea Alliance era. Netiwit is a Buddhist, Chow a Catholic, and Diamond a Muslim. As I write this, in October 2024, Netiwit is the only one of the three who is still living in the place of his birth. Diamond is in exile in Konstanz, Germany. Chow is pursuing a master's degree at the University of Toronto.

What unites these three are shared strategies and objectives that knit them and many other activists together into the Milk Tea Alliance. The Milk Tea Alliance, of course, extends far beyond these three figures, and includes activists from across Asia, many of whom cannot be fully covered within the scope of this book. But the experiences of Chow, Netiwit, and Diamond encapsulate the challenges faced by countless others within the movement.

The Milk Tea Alliance is a loose, decentralized network of companions among hundreds or even thousands of activists. It is just one of the ways participants identify themselves, serving more as an umbrella term, similar to "the counterculture" in the 1960s rather than as one of the specific organizational names used for youths groups during that decade. We don't know whether a hundred years from now this period of Asian protest movements will be referred to as the Milk Tea Alliance era. Or if a new configuration emerges, it may be seen as having laid the groundwork, the way that civil society activities across the Soviet bloc in the 1960s and 1970s did for the struggles of 1989. But a shared sense of aspirations and values gives it at least the potential of becoming a significant movement that evolves and gains more traction over time.

The primary goal of Milk Tea Alliance activists is to see their communities governed in a more just and democratic fashion. They champion fundamental rights such as free elections, free speech, free assembly, and civil liberties. The activists do not engage extensively with questions of governance post-revolution, instead maintaining a narrower focus on opposing authoritarianism and countering the global, bullying influence of the Chinese Communist Party. Achieving these objectives is an extraordinarily challenging task, which underscores the remarkable resilience and determination of its members in the face of overwhelming odds.

After engaging with numerous Milk Tea Alliance activists, their optimism and unwavering belief in change—even if it may take a long time or require an unexpected shift in the elite, as with Mikhail Gorbachev's rise to power in Moscow, or when death removes certain "old men" from the scene—is undeniably infectious. By highlighting the courage and resolve of just a few alliance members, I am left with a profound sense of hope—that a new generation has risen to confront the region's drift toward authoritarianism. These activists deeply believe in the possibility of a better future even in dark times, and it is their collective courage that sustains this vision.

Thailand

It is midway through a warm spring morning in Norway in 2018 when Netiwit takes the stage in a packed theater. He is in Oslo to give a talk titled "The Student vs. The Military" that will use incidents from his life to back up his arguments about the problems plaguing Thailand, a country whose path toward becoming a stable democracy keeps being derailed by coups. The young activist, who is studying political science at Bangkok's prestigious Chulalongkorn University and is deeply versed in both Buddhism and theories of civil disobedience, plans to outline some of the changes he feels are needed to get the country heading in the right direction, including doing away with military conscription. The presentation by Thailand's first conscientious objector will be one of several on this second of three days of the tenth annual Oslo Freedom Forum.

One of the first things the audience notices about Netiwit is his distinctive red glasses with rectangular plastic frames. Some say they give him a studious look, while his friends describe them as "nerdy"—a label he embraces, as his "nerdy" appearance mirrors that of Hong Kong activist Joshua Wong. This resemblance could be a sign that the two were meant to be friends.

As a compulsive reader, Netiwit takes words seriously. He has been laboring over each line, knowing that he needs to keep his TED-talk-style speech concise, between ten and fifteen minutes, so every word has to count. For a strong opening, he settles on this: "I could not come to this place if I had been arrested with my friends who went to demonstration [sic] on the fourth anniversary of the coup."

Besides a welcome by a North Korean defector, the event features talks by other activists, such as Vanessa Berhe on Eritrea ("One Day Seyoum") and Edipcia Dubón on Nicaragua ("Unmasking Ortega's Regime"). This kind of programming, typical for the forum, takes the audience on a global tour that emphasizes repression and resistance over natural or architectural marvels, focusing more on historical massacres than museums. The presenters, often witnesses to brutality by the authorities, share distressing and deeply personal accounts of human rights abuses, along with inspiring stories of individuals and groups fighting to end these injustices.

Netiwit is particularly struck by how, despite the language barrier, every member of the crowd seems captivated by Dubón's story. They listen closely as she describes the tragic turn in her homeland, which, after a hopeful period, has once again fallen under a dictator's control—a fate all too familiar in a country with a long history of strongmen. Certain parts of her story resonate deeply with his own.

Thailand is a large and consequential place. It is home to close to 70 million people. It is one of the four biggest countries in

Southeast Asia by area. And it boasts the region's second-largest economy. However, international media coverage often focuses more on its appeal as a tourist destination—highlighting its beaches and cuisine—rather than its political landscape.

One reason is that even when things are going badly there, they are even worse for its neighbors. Thailand has periodically been under military rule, including the government at that time, led by General Prayuth Chan-ocha, who initially assumed power as a junta leader and now serves as Prime Minister. But when people think about the most troubled countries in Southeast Asia, others come to mind first. Laos is a severely oppressive state, and Cambodia is still recovering from one of the worst genocides in history. Then there is Burma, where a program of ethnic cleansing is being directed at the Rohingya people.

Earlier Netiwit had met and taken an instant liking to Zoya Phan, a Burmese activist in her late thirties, and Mu Sochua, a Cambodian activist in her mid-sixties. Both of them have been taking big risks to work for change in their countries. But Netiwit believes Thai activists deserve global attention, respect, and encouragement, even if their situation is not as dire. It may be a hard sell in a setting like the Freedom Forum, in which some members of the audience continue to view the world through Cold War categories. Thailand is not thought of as part of a dangerous bloc, never having been under Communist rule and having long been a US ally. But Netiwit is deeply concerned by the way that, lately, Bangkok and Beijing have grown close, with the junta sending a large group of Uyghurs who had sought refuge in Thailand back to the Chinese mainland at the request of the Chinese Communist Party.

The presence of veteran activist Fang Zheng holds special significance for Netiwit, given his interest in Beijing's human rights record. Fang, a fifty-one-year-old Chinese dissident in exile, has been confined to a wheelchair since soldiers opened fire on protesters and bystanders, and tanks rolled through central Beijing in early June 1989.

Netiwit believes that Thailand is being held back from becoming a fully democratic and open country by a set of outdated and interconnected militaristic and hierarchical practices. The country was supposed to have changed from an absolutist monarchy to a constitutional one in 1932, a time it also began to be known as Thailand rather than Siam (a shift of nomenclature formalized in 1939). The transition was never completed, though, due to shifting coalitions of members of the conservative business elite, the military, and the royal family. These coalitions have worked in different combinations, often aided by the courts, to derail liberalizers. Time and again, coups derail progress toward a sustainable form of democracy. Elections take place, but it is never clear how long the winner will be able to serve without the result being nullified by yet another coup.

Coups are not the only thing that have kept progressive forces in check, Netiwit and those with similar views know. Also important is the way that the police and the courts apply harsh and vaguely defined regulations against defaming the royal family, which is a crime under Section 112 of the Thai criminal code. Sometimes known simply as "112," lèse-majesté laws make it a high crime to insult the king and queen, or even to discuss the role of the royal family in politics, since this is seen as raising doubts about the monarchy's legitimacy.

When speaking in public in the past, Netiwit has had to shout to be heard or use undependable amplifiers and static-prone handheld mics. Fortunately, he has been fitted with a state-of-the-art hands-free mic, which will make it easier to end his talk by inviting the audience to join him in holding up three-fingers in a salute of resistance. This gesture, like so many things that matter to Netiwit, has its roots in books—in this case, Suzanne Collins's dystopian *Hunger Games* novels. In the story, the salute originates in one region under autocratic rule and is later adopted by young people across the land who stand up against a brutal regime. Against overwhelming odds, they ultimately toppled the tyrant. The gesture's popularity is largely due to the films based on the books, where, in a memorable scene, Jennifer Lawrence's character, the reluctant rebel Katniss, uses the salute in a ceremony honoring a fallen comrade. Later it becomes a symbol of solidarity and defiance for the people.

In 2014, one of the *Hunger Games* movies was playing in theaters when the military again took control of Thailand. Youths began incorporating the three-finger salute into protests against real-life autocrats, whom they saw as resembling the villains in the film. Authorities responded by arresting people for making the gesture. That same year, the salute appeared in protests in Hong Kong, with some viewing young activist Agnes Chow as the city's very own Katniss.

Netiwit jokes that even though the junta punishes people in Thailand for holding up three fingers, he thinks it will be safe for them to join him in making the gesture here in Norway, far from the junta's reach. The joke works. There is laughter as people throughout the theater show solidarity with Netiwit.

He is glad he decided to end the talk this way, and he chalks it up as another example of how friendship and activism have complemented one another in his life, because the idea came from his new friends from Cambodia and Burma.

Netiwit was born in 1996 in central Thailand to parents who ran a vegetarian grocery store and divorced when he was young. They were not elite, but also not completely disadvantaged, and Netiwit claims that his life was not all that different from that of the average boy raised in a lower-middle-class family.

When Netiwit was fourteen, he attended a temple gathering and heard a talk by Sulak Sivaraksa, one of Thailand's leading Buddhist figures. Sulak has been a controversial fixture of the country's political and cultural scene for decades. Netiwit was so impressed that he went to hear Sulak speak a second time, and sought him out as a mentor. Sulak has deep connections with Tibetan exiles and is an old friend of the Dalai Lama's, so it wasn't a surprise that Netiwit inherited Sulak's antipathy toward Beijing due to its policies in Tibet. Netiwit has been studying with and working with Sulak ever since.

It was around this time that Netiwit got his first taste of organizing by co-founding a group called the Thailand Education Revolution Alliance. In 2013, a year before graduating high school, Netiwit began protesting a rule at Thai schools requiring teenage boys to keep their hair in a short, army-style cut. School officials reprimanded him at length, and this made the news. All of a sudden, he was being interviewed by the Thai press and even by some international reporters. It was a lot for a sixteen-year-old to handle, but he was not completely unprepared. Sulak was a veteran at engaging with the media, so Netiwit had someone to turn to for advice. Protests like Netiwit's were rare, which made them newsworthy. But many Thais were already feeling that democracy would always be a precarious thing if military values pervaded society.

At the time, Thailand was in a rare period of elected civilian rule, but there were ominous signs that suggested this might not last. Competing crowds wearing different-colored shirts began to fill the streets of Bangkok day after day. Those sporting red shirts came out to support Yingluck Shinawatra, the first woman to ever serve as the country's Prime Minister. The Pheu Thai party that she led had swept the 2011 national election. Those sporting yellow shirts called for her resignation. Reporters asked the head of the Royal Thai Army, General Prayuth, what he would do if the conflict continued. He refused to rule out using force to restore order. The situation was tense, since Thailand had previously been shaken by a dozen successful coups, as well as many failed ones. There had been one as recently as 2006, which ended with a general backed by the royal family replacing an elected civilian as the head of the government and imposing martial law. The person that coup unseated was Yingluk's brother, Thaksin Shinawatra, who had been elected Prime Minister in 2001, as head of the Thai Rak Thai Party, a precursor to Pheu Thai.

Thaksin was a charismatic and controversial business magnate who had ruffled the feathers of the military, conservative tycoons, and the royal family. He was disliked not just by these defenders of the traditional establishment but also by some anti-establishment Bangkok intellectuals, including Sulak, who called Thaksin a "crook" and a "dictator in the guise of democracy" in a 2010 interview. But Thaksin had long had a broad base of support in the countryside, especially among poor villagers who were drawn to his populist programs that promised to improve their economic lot. They saw him as an outsider who was finally trying to do something about the gross disparities of wealth and poverty in the country. His sister had inherited his base of support.

The general behind the 2006 coup had pushed the elder Shinawatra sibling from power. Thaksin was forced into exile to avoid serving a long prison sentence for corruption charges that he insisted were politically motivated. He maintained his popularity among the rural poor. When his political party was outlawed, it was reconfigured as Pheu Thai, with his sister Yingluk as its head. She managed to get along with the royal family better than her brother had, but there continued to be rifts with the establishment. As crowds clashed late in 2013, it seemed that 2014 might witness a repetition of 2006, just with a different member of the family falling and fleeing.

As the situation on the streets grew tenser and tenser, Netiwit was becoming active in a broader educational reform campaign whose goal was to make Thailand's treatment of children less militaristic. "School is like a factory that manufactures identical people," Netiwit told the *New York Times*. He joined with other high school students in this effort, and there were also some college students who made common cause with them, including Piyarat "Toto" Chongthep, who would become a frequent ally.

During this time, Netiwit delved into the world of American protest songs, and developed a love for the music of Pete Seeger, a legendary banjo-playing singer-songwriter and progressive activist. Netiwit had first become aware of Seeger while watching documentaries on the Civil Rights Movement. His favorite song was "We Shall Overcome," a spiritual which Seeger and others adapted from an earlier one called "We Will Overcome" and that Seeger popularized, singing it as a protest song in civil rights marches. It had circled the globe and shown up in all sorts of movements, and was even sung in a protest in Thailand in the 1970s. Netiwit learned that the title had shown up on a t-shirt in a famous photograph of a youth who took part in 1989's Tiananmen Square protest in Beijing, and that the words rang out in Prague during that same year's Velvet Revolution. He also learned that Seeger sang at Quaker events and was deeply involved with the community, meaning that he, like Netiwit, was a pacificist for reasons related to religion. Netiwit became obsessed with Seeger, and sought out all the Seeger recordings he could find in Bangkok.

Early in 2014 news of Seeger's death reached Netiwit, and he and two like-minded friends organized a Bangkok memorial concert for the American. The concert drew a small crowd who were each given a leaflet with a few paragraphs Netiwit wrote extolling the virtues of Seeger as a "noble singer" and encouraging them to join in singing along with a band. Some of those who came, including Toto, would go on to become leading figures in Thailand's dissident scene, some doing so while staying within the country's borders, as Netiwit and Toto have done, and others as political exiles driven to seek safety abroad to avoid long prison terms for allegedly violating lèse-majesté laws.

Days later, Netiwit set off to study at a school in the Himalayas that his mentor chose for him. Sulak, admired for his commitment to social justice and criticized by some for his support of the monarchy, is best known internationally for his role in the Engaged Buddhism movement. A collaboration among socially conscious Buddhists across Asia, the movement takes its name from a term first used by Vietnamese peace activist Thích Nhất Hạnh in the early 1960s. It became an important pan-Asian force in the 1970s, thanks in part to the connections its Vietnamese founders made with like-minded figures based everywhere from India to Taiwan and Thailand, and it shares similarities with the Milk Tea Alliance in which Netiwit would later become active.

Sulak titled his autobiography *Loyalty Demands Dissent*, and in it he describes an approach to taking stands on principles that is rooted in the idea that one simply wants to see the representatives of the current structure live up to their own ideals. Netiwit has never had to leave the country to avoid lèse-majesté prosecution, but his mentor has had to do that more than once. This is true even though Sulak has consistently insisted that he is pro-royalist in his political views. He simply feels that being pro-royalist should not get in the way of noting when the monarchy doesn't live up to expectations. And crucially, Sulak is opposed to Thailand's system of mandatory military conscription.

Netiwit was born into a Buddhist household in a country where Buddhism is prevalent, but he became devout when he decided to follow Sulak. Like Sulak, Netiwit is a pacifist who believes changing the world for the better is possible, and they both look for strategies that could help improve Thailand wherever they could be found, including in struggles and writings associated with foreign writers and other parts of the world.

He was eager to take a real trip abroad, and India was where Gandhi, a figure who fascinated and inspired him, had been born. Long before that it was where the Buddha himself had lived. Netiwit is part of a family with ancestral ties to China, but he had never ventured out of Thailand. He was ready to move from armchair travel to the real thing.

On May 22, 2014, General Prayuth made good on his threat and staged a coup to overthrow Yingluck's government. Prayuth quickly formed a military junta that instituted laws banning all public gatherings of more than a few people. Taylor Swift canceled her planned appearance in Bangkok due to the coup. A theater in the northern city of Chiang Mai was pressured into canceling a scheduled screening of a film version of George Orwell's *1984*. Some protesters responded by unfurling a banner portraying Prayuth as Thailand's Big Brother.

Around the same time, the latest installment of the cinematic *Hunger Games* series was opening in Thai movie theaters. Since the first book's release in 2008, *The Hunger Games* series had gained a global readership and was quickly translated into many languages, including Thai. The four Hollywood films further amplified the impact of this story about young, determined rebels overthrowing a powerful dictatorship.

In both Thailand and Hong Kong, where the Umbrella Movement was underway when the movie came out, some youths inspired by the spirit of the film began to flash three-finger salutes, and the gesture was picked up in Burma, too.* The use of the salute cast the authorities the youths challenged into the

---

* In 2015, Burmese activists protested Beijing's involvement in a controversial copper mine, which was criticized for exploiting workers. During the unauthorized demonstration outside the Chinese embassy in Yangon, a Chinese flag was burned. Six of the activists were sentenced to fifty-two months in prison, and as they were escorted out of the courtroom, they raised the three-finger salute, which was documented in Elliott Prasse-Freeman's *Rights Refused: Grassroots Activism and State Violence in Myanmar* (Stanford University Press, 2023, pp. 17–18).

role of tyrants. At first, the authorities did not know enough to appreciate the subversiveness of the gesture. Soon, though, they caught on and banned the movie, and the salute was criminalized.

Despite yet another coup, there were no major calls for international companies to rethink their investments in Thailand and no major effort to get tourists to stop traveling there. After some statements decrying the coup, most foreign countries quickly resumed business as usual with Bangkok. This was partly due to the frequency of coups in Thailand—at least a dozen since the 1930s—and partly due to the symbolic continuity provided by King Bhumibol, who had ascended to the throne in 1946 at the age of nineteen, and was popular with the people, respected internationally, and appeared comfortable with Prayuth in power and the streets free of demonstrators.

News of this coup, and of Yingluk following her brother Thaksin into exile, rattled Netiwit when it reached him in Bir, India. His program at the Deerpark Institute was supposed to involve long hours immersed in religious texts and studying Sanskrit to better understand Buddhist works. He also studied to improve his English, because he wanted to get a better sense of news from around the world and read more widely in philosophy. But the coup shook him, and he had heard that students back in Bangkok, including Toto, who was studying at Thammasat University, were struggling to find ways to express their outrage over the coup. He began reading about civil disobedience because it would help him find ways to contribute on his return.

Netiwit got to know an elderly Tibetan Buddhist nun who had been living in India for decades. She told him chilling tales about China's Communist Party. After promising Tibetans in the early 1950s that they could enjoy a lot of autonomy as a special sort of protected part of the People's Republic of China, the Party had destroyed temples and brutalized believers across her homeland. The Dalai Lama had initially thought he could work with Chairman Mao and other Communist leaders, but things got so bad that he fled to India in 1959. After that, Beijing worked to undermine the activities and sully the reputation of His Holiness. These tales led Netiwit to seek out articles and books on Beijing's repressive moves, reading on topics such as the massacre of protesters and bystanders near Tiananmen Square in 1989.

If it was inspiration he was seeking, he found it in a powerful collection of essays by a famous figure from the Chinese mainland: Liu Xiaobo. Liu was a political prisoner and, like Martin Luther King, Jr., a Nobel Peace Prize Laureate. The volume filled with Liu's essays and poems that Netiwit read was called *No Enemies, No Hatred*, a title that resonated with his spiritual convictions. An added plus was that it came with a foreword by someone he had not read before, but who would join King in Netiwit's personal pantheon of revered thinkers from faraway lands. This was Václav Havel, who decades before the Velvet Revolution had been part of 1968's Prague Spring and nine years after that had been the key figure in the "Charter 77" drive. That drive had in turn inspired Liu and his collaborators to create "Charter 08," a Chinese counterpart calling for expanded civil liberties and freedom of expression in a country under Communist Party rule.

Thailand's many coups often led to brief periods of junta rule. But Prayuth governed for nearly a decade, backed by a coalition of fellow generals, the royal family, and conservative business elites. Meanwhile, in 2014 the international news cycle moved on to protests and repression in other parts of the world. In August, Americans took to the streets against racism and police violence after the killing of Black teenager Michael Brown in Ferguson, Missouri. In September, the dramatic Umbrella Movement for democracy and fair elections began in Hong Kong.

In 1997, Hong Kong, which had long been a British colony, became a Special Administrative Region of the People's Republic of China. Beijing made its residents a promise much like the one it made Tibetans decades earlier, saying they could largely go their own way under a setup known as "One Country, Two Systems." The idea was for Hong Kong's people to defer to Beijing in some matters, such as diplomacy, but maintain a distinctive way of life. There was tension baked into this arrangement from the start: Beijing wanted the city to stay different in economic regards but conform in others, while many locals valued the city's distinctive legal system and freer press.

Netiwit read everything that he could find about the Umbrella Movement, which was so named because protesters found umbrellas to be effective against the police's use of pepper spray. A *TIME* magazine cover story that helped solidify the name in the global imagination made a deep impression on Netiwit. Published as the movement's center of gravity shifted from the original, older organizers of Occupy Central to younger activists, the story focused on Joshua Wong, whom *TIME* dubbed the face of Hong Kong's struggle for democracy. Wong was committed to non-violence, but he also advocated for more militant and controversial actions within a non-violent framework than the movement's founders had initially envisioned.

Netiwit had already heard about Wong two years before, when Wong and his schoolmates pushed back against Beijing's efforts to bring their city more in line with mainland patterns of life. It was a much larger movement than the one at Netiwit's school, and he was amazed at what they had accomplished. They had managed to ensure that among other things, Hong Kong teachers could still teach in detail about subjects that were skated over or treated as completely taboo on the mainland, such as the history of the Tiananmen protests and June Fourth Massacre. This was an effort to maintain the "two systems" part of "One Country, Two Systems." Each year, people in Hong Kong and Macau—but not in any other mainland Chinese cities—could commemorate the martyrs of 1989 with a candlelight vigil.

In 2014, Wong and other young activists had a broader goal: making Hong Kong fully democratic. When it was a British colony, the top official was a governor appointed from London. It had become more democratic late in the colonial era, when an elected legislature had some power, but it was still run by someone who was neither ethnically Chinese nor answerable to voters. By 2014, the government was headed by a Chief Executive who was ethnically Chinese, but chosen through a convoluted process in which only candidates approved by a nominating committee could run—a structure designed to ensure the Chief Executive was always acceptable to Beijing.

For weeks, the struggle succeeded in mobilizing tens of thousands of people for action. But in the end the Umbrella Movement failed to achieve its main goal. But Netiwit had no doubt that he could learn much from Wong, and he felt they had a lot in common. Wong, like Netiwit, was a person of faith, and they had both become activists in high school. They were born about a month apart.

In 2016, Netiwit finally came up with an excuse to reach out to Wong. He sent Wong an email inviting him to speak in Bangkok. But he received no response. So he flew to Hong Kong in July and showed up at a campaign rally staged by a new party Wong and his friends had started. He introduced himself to the youth he had come to feel was a kindred spirit, almost a doppelganger, and convinced Wong to go out for a meal with him. After a couple of hours together, they became fast friends.

Early in October, Wong flew to Bangkok to take up Netiwit's invitation. The idea was to have Wong, who had taken part in Hong Kong commemorations of the 1989 massacre near Tiananmen Square, help mark the fortieth anniversary of the infamous 1976 massacre at Bangkok's Thammasat University. But Thai officials, at the urging of Beijing, took away Wong's phone and detained him at the airport for twelve hours. Neither Netiwit nor any of Wong's Hong Kong friends knew what was happening to him. Then the authorities sent Wong back to Hong Kong—he didn't even set foot outside the airport.

The incident came on the heels of other forms of collusion between Bangkok and Beijing authorities, such as Thai authorities sending Uyghurs seeking refuge in Thailand back to China. It shed light on a shift in international relations: after decades as a staunch American ally, Thailand was getting closer and closer to China in diplomatic terms. Thailand maintained good relations with Washington and enjoyed its support, but the United States had balked at the coup and expressed concern about it before deciding to continue working with the new government. Beijing had not shown any similar scruples.

In personal rather than diplomatic terms, the incident cemented Netiwit and Wong's friendship. They had a common enemy in the Chinese Communist Party. When Netiwit and some friends gathered in Bangkok to call for the detained Wong to be released, they held up umbrellas to signify their solidarity with Hong Kong.

When Netiwit returned home from India, he enrolled in Chulalongkorn University to study political science. Chula, as it is often called, was the first university to be established in Thailand by its namesake, the Thai king who laid the groundwork for the country's intended path toward Westernization. With a sprawling campus located in the heart of the city's shopping areas as opposed to near its political center, the university's royal connection and origins as an institution designed to train royal pages and bureaucrats cemented a reputation of muted political apathy and conservatism. Even the choice of pink as the university's signature color had a tie to the monarchy, as it was the auspicious color of the day King Chulalongkorn was born.

The start of college was not the only milestone for Netiwit. He was about to turn eighteen, which is the age when young men in Thailand are required to register for the draft. A college student like Netiwit would have been eligible for an exemption, but this was a matter of principle for him, and he published an open letter proclaiming that he would not register. This was the action that led to him being called his country's first official conscientious objector. He claimed that serving in the armed forces went against his Buddhist beliefs, but it was part of a larger opposition to the military's place in Thai society.

Many young men with connected parents find ways to get around serving as soldiers. But refusing to register was unprecedented. Netiwit knew this. He also knew, though, that there were precedents in other places for his action. He knew of a long tradition within Buddhism of opposing all forms of war. "Everyone is a human being; I do not kill anyone," he wrote. "I will be a 'conscientious objector,' I will not be a soldier in the Thai army or any violent army." He also saw his actions as placing him in a lineage that included Americans who burned their draft cards.

As far back as his time in secondary school, Netiwit had won an election to a school government post (by a "landslide," at least according to one newspaper), helped found two student reform associations, and took a leading role in an educational reform journal. The authorities at his secondary school grew so frustrated with his objections to their rules that they stripped him of his student government post.

At Chula, Netiwit joined another classmate in refusing to perform a campus ritual in the required way. During an initiation ceremony, all first-year students were supposed to prostrate themselves in front of the statue of Rama V, or King Chulalongkorn, the school's namesake, and pledge an oath to uphold the school's principles and revere the royal family. But these two freshmen greeted the statue not kneeling but standing up, and looking the sovereign in the eye. Netiwit had read in a book that Chulalongkorn himself, wanting to act as a modern monarch, had said his subjects should not grovel before him like serfs, and had abolished prostration.

A year later, Netiwit protested the same ritual with even more drama. A few months after he won a student election to become the head of the Chula Student Council, he led a group walkout during the campus ritual, with several other council members joining him in boycotting the event. This walkout had a dramatic immediate effect. A professor grabbed a Council member and roughly held him in a headlock.

The walkout also had a broader effect within the school. Students all need to maintain good "behavioral scores" to hold offices in government, and the scores of the activists were all cut as a punishment for their transgression. Carina Chotirawe, a Chula professor sympathetic to the activists, suggested that the "dismissals from the student council were less about misconduct than undermining what Netiwit represents." Netiwit was just one of the people stripped of their posts, but his status as the leader of the protest soon became clear.

Prime Minister Prayuth, speaking at another university, singled Netiwit out for criticism. Even though he did not say Netiwit's name, he said that the election of a certain person to head the Chula student government was a "disgrace" to not just the institution but to the nation.

Netiwit responded with a Facebook post saying that the real "disgrace" to Thailand was that General Prayuth had never been elected to anything, since the junta had consistently rebuffed demands that they hold a new national election, and yet he had taken on the title of Prime Minister. Netiwit had close to 50,000 Facebook followers, and after the general's criticism was reported in the Thai press, his social media following grew even larger. *Reuters* published an article that described Netiwit as a "rare critic of the military junta" and noted that some drew comparisons between him and Joshua Wong.

Netiwit and the student protesters appealed the way the administration had punished them. In October, they all called for the behavior point deductions to be reversed, their positions on the Council restored, and for investigation into the action of the professor who put the student in a chokehold. To add pressure to these efforts, the group secured signatures from 150 high-profile international scholars, scientists, writers, and activists from 60 institutions in 19 countries on an open letter calling for a reversal of the actions against the students. Signatories included Noam Chomsky, Steven Pinker, social theorist James C. Scott, China specialists Jean-Philippe Béja and Perry Link, Indian public intellectual Ashis Nandy, feminist philosopher Judith Butler, and historian Timothy Snyder.

The publishing bug had bitten Netiwit. He joined with some of his Chula classmates to establish Sam Yan Press, named for a neighborhood near Chula. Netiwit and his colleagues take turns translating foreign works into Thai, sometimes working on their own and sometimes in pairs or small groups. They view this as a way to do their bit to provide the people of Thailand, and its youth in particular, with tools that will help in the long run to undermine and dismantle the military-capitalist-monarchical establishment that holds their country back.

The first volume Sam Yan brought out was a collection of writings on civil disobedience by a mix of international figures. Some of these, such as King's "Letter from Birmingham Jail," were translated by Netiwit, and the book was a birthday present for Wong, who was about to turn twenty-one in prison. The volume was meant to help Wong keep his spirits up until he was out of jail.

The press has published many works by people who signed the open letter, including a book by Butler on non-violence, Snyder's *On Tyranny: Twenty Lessons from the Twentieth Century*, a work that made the author globally famous when it became a bestseller in the wake of Donald Trump's 2016 victory, and Scott's *Two Cheers for Anarchism*.

In 2019, Thailand had its first election since the coup. Some former student activists ran for Parliament as members of a new progressive party, Future Forward. The party performed well, but it was forced to disband soon afterward as the establishment used compliant courts to undermine the organization, and the leaders of the party were banned from running for office.

The banning of Future Forward ignited the country's biggest wave of protests this century, as university students led massive demonstrations against General Prayuth and the Thai monarchy. In Hong Kong, after one last giant New Year's Day march, public gatherings largely disappeared because of rules during the COVID pandemic. In the summer of 2020, Beijing imposed a draconian new National Security Law on the city, which meant one could be punished severely for organizing collective actions. To date, nearly three hundred activists have been arrested under the law, and political dissent has been all but silenced in Hong Kong. When the massive movement began in Thailand in 2020, it was as if a baton had been passed from Hong Kong to Bangkok.

In April 2020, some activists in both cities began to refer to themselves as members of the "Milk Tea Alliance" and express a commitment to support each other's struggles. A few months later, when Chula students posted on social media about their demonstrations and needing to learn to defend themselves from the pepper spray and tear gas police were using against them, some Hong Kong activists arranged to send them a gift of raincoats and goggles that they had used on the streets in 2019 but now had no use for in a city effectively under martial law. The Chula students reciprocated by holding a campus vigil on June 4 to honor the Beijing martyrs of 1989.

James Buchanan, who has written about the protests in both cities, uses the term "protest swapping" to refer to such exchanges. There were other examples. Bunkueanun "Francis" Paothong, a twenty-year-old student inspired by the Milk Tea Alliance, organized a small protest outside Bangkok's Chinese Embassy and sang "Glory to Hong Kong," a song that was by then illegal to sing in public in its eponymous locale, on China's National Day in 2020. (A year before there had been mass protests in Hong Kong, and the Hong Kong police fired live ammunition after months of deploying tear gas and rubber bullets.) The next month, as police brutality became an increasingly important part of what kept Bangkok protests swelling, Joshua Wong also protest swapped, as he stood outside the Thai consulate in Hong Kong and denounced repression in Thailand. That protest would be one of his last public acts: he was arrested soon afterward and has not been at liberty since.

The Milk Tea Alliance expanded into neighboring Burma when activists began mass demonstrations against the brutal coup that curtailed democratization in February 2021. In solidarity, Thai activists, by now following a familiar script, gathered outside Burma's Embassy in Bangkok in protest.

The term Milk Tea Alliance grew out of a very specific set of early 2020 online clashes. The drama began with social media posts by a celebrity known to fans as "Bright" who starred in a Thai "boys love" series (a genre celebrating male same sex romantic storylines) that was popular in various parts of East and Southeast Asia. He "liked" a post that referred to Hong Kong as one of four "countries," and this infuriated some intensely nationalistic internet users on the Chinese mainland. They called for him to apologize. Around the same time, Bright's girlfriend, also a celebrity, referred to Taiwan in a manner that suggested it should be treated as its own entity.

There had been many incidents just prior to this where objections had led to apologies from celebrities who were reluctant to alienate mainland consumers or to be blocked from the Chinese market. Some of these successful online campaigns had targeted companies that used maps on their websites that had Taiwan a different color than the People's Republic of China. Others had called on celebrities to retract statements praising the Dalia Lama, since Communist Party-run media insists that he is an immoral promoter of separatist views. When Hong Kong's pop star Denise Ho became an outspoken supporter of the Umbrella Movement, she stopped being able to tour on the mainland, where she had a lot of fans, and her songs were blocked by mainland streaming services. A French cosmetics firm, bowing to pressure from Beijing, stopped using her as a pitch person for their products across East Asia. Undaunted, she continued to support Hong Kong activists, and she is currently awaiting trial on politically motivated charges in the city, her passport taken from her so she is no longer able to travel.

When Bright and his girlfriend faced online pressure to apologize for their posts, fans of the couple, based in Taiwan and Hong Kong as well as their native Thailand, called for the pair to stand firm.

The goal of Milk Tea Alliance members, as defenders of the couple soon began to call themselves, was to unite people from different parts of Asia who were not just critical of autocracy where they lived but were equally concerned about the Chinese Communist Party's repressive domestic policies, its pattern of colluding with nearby dictators, and its efforts to control political discourse.

The idea behind the Milk Tea Alliance was to use online expressions of solidarity to support people across the region with similar goals, as well as to share ideas about tactics and strategies. The organization's playful name was rooted in the popularity of Hong Kong milk tea, which is highly caffeinated and sweetened with condensed milk; bubble tea in Taiwan, which is filled with tapioca called boba as well as milk; and Thai tea, which is very sweet and like its Hong Kong counterpart made with condensed milk and sometimes evaporated milk as well.

To express their support, Netiwit, Wong, and other like-minded youth began filling their social media accounts with comments praising the Milk Tea Alliance. They also reposted memes showing animated cups of the three types of tea swearing loyalty to one another, evoking the "all for one, and one for all" spirit of *The Three Musketeers* and the sworn brotherhoods of traditional Chinese novels featuring bandits and rebels.

By the summer of 2020, the student protests that began after the Thai regime had dissolved the Future Forward Party were coalescing into a massive movement that not only criticized the military, but was beginning to deal with the biggest taboo in the country: challenging the Thai monarchy. During an event in front of a small crowd, speakers indirectly criticized the Thai regime by comparing them to the villain Voldemort, a form of deniability as well as playful critique of the King and other powerful figures that Thai activists had used before. But then a thirty-six-year-old human rights lawyer named Anon Nampa got up to speak and shocked the audience when he moved from playfulness to directly calling for change in the role of the monarchy.

Few could have predicted that the central figure in the movement would be a bespectacled student of Thammasat University who had an unassuming demeanor. She was twenty-one, studious, and often described herself as being shy by nature. But when Panusaya "Rung" Sithijirawattanakul, wearing a simple red dress, strode onto a stage in front of several thousand of her peers on a steamy August day and moved up to the microphone to speak, she made history.

Rung, which means "rainbow," read out a manifesto that she and some colleagues had drafted that included a ten-point program to reform the monarchy. These were the kinds of demands that exiles talked about from the safety of abroad. Rung's calls for greater accountability and decriminalizing criticism of the monarchy might not have seemed radical in many parts of the world that still have kings or queens on thrones but have parliaments and other elected bodies as well that wield great power. In Thailand, however, to give this kind of speech was to challenge a venerated pillar of the nation. It was, for some, tantamount to treason.

Her speech was the first in living memory in which someone speaking on Thai soil before a big crowd dared to openly call for drastic changes in the country's powerful system of kingship. The risks she was taking by speaking in this way were clear: people had paid with jail time or forced exile for saying far less on the topic, others with their lives.

Rung quickly became the face of the movement, and as she gave speeches in front of larger and larger crowds, she was eventually arrested on lèse-majesté and other charges. Her photograph appeared often in newspapers. In many shots, she is shown holding up three fingers on one of her hands. A Bangkok-based periodical designated her the country's "Person of the Year," after she had been a mainstay at many of the biggest marches in Bangkok in recent history.

Netiwit marched in some of these, too. Sometimes, though, he used demonstrations as occasions to set up bookstalls on the protest route, encouraging people to purchase copies of Sam Yan books to read after the protest. On a couple of occasions, he helped integrate Sam Yan books into protests. The group's translation of Hannah Arendt's "Personal Responsibility Under Dictatorship" (an essay published as a book in Thai) was incorporated into a piece of dissident performance art, for example. And aphorisms from Snyder's *On Tyranny* were printed out and held up by protesters.

In addition, Netiwit invited Rung to speak at Chula, a campus with long ties to the royal family. And this time, in contrast to what happened when he invited Wong, he succeeded in hosting a controversial figure. It was among other things a symbolic act to show that Chula and Thammasat should both be seen as radical hubs. Chula again stripped Netiwit of his student council presidency. It is perhaps just a wonder that his alma mater's administrators never went further and tried to get this perennial thorn in their side expelled; he stayed at the school until graduating earlier this year.

When I visited Thailand for the first time in the middle of 2022, I was hoping to meet Netiwit. This was impossible, though, as he was preparing to enter a period of seclusion as a monk in a Buddhist monastery.

My hosts for my campus visit were two students: a young woman who goes by the nickname Mew, and a young man named Krittapas Chedjaroenrat. The two were close colleagues of Netiwit's who had helped take charge of operations at the publishing house in his absence. Krittapas gave me a set of postcards the youths had made, covered with images and slogans associated with the Milk Tea Alliance, mixed in with quotations from figures associated with resistance from outside of Asia, including Nelson Mandela and Martin Luther King, Jr. He also showed me a pair of socks that the group was particularly proud to be distributing. On the toe of one foot, there was an image of a Thai general. On the toe of the other foot, there was an image of a Burmese general. When Krittapas held up the socks, one of the other students started giggling and this proved infectious; soon all of them were laughing. I found the socks amusing, too—a clever way of mocking powerful people and suggesting that the rulers of Thailand and Burma were the same sorts of bullies.

Spending time in a monastery is a common way for young men to avoid the military draft, so by the next year Netiwit had cut short his stint, as he didn't want to be protected from prosecution as a conscientious objector. He wanted to show that he was fully prepared to spend time in prison.

Netiwit and his colleagues have been devoting a lot of their energy to an off-campus but still Chula-related activity. This is an anti-gentrification campaign whose goal is to protect small businesses in the Sam Yan neighborhood. The campaign centers on efforts to save a modest but beloved traditional Chinese shrine near the university from being bulldozed to make room for luxury condos that are part of a development drive backed by Chula's administration. When a documentary about the shrine titled *The Last Breath of Sam Yan* was released to good reviews and began to be accepted for showings at film festivals, Netiwit's name appeared in the credits as a co-producer.

Netiwit and other members of the Sam Yan publishing group even collaborated with local chefs in launching a restaurant that specializes in Burmese noodle dishes. It is called Delicious Democracy and operates on the ground floor of the building where the press has its headquarters. The walls are covered with political art and there is a shelf displaying new Sam Yan titles above the dining tables. The dishes are made following recipes used at a local eatery that was forced to close. The Sam Yan group initially wanted to get the chefs of that restaurant to run this one, but when those chefs found other jobs before this could be arranged, the campaign found other staff to step in who agreed to follow the old recipes.

I finally met Netiwit during a visit to Bangkok early in 2024. The late afternoon began at Delicious Democracy, with me eating samosas and talking with colleagues of Netiwit's. Then he joined us, and we kept conversing as we walked through the neighborhood. One topic that came up was the way that fissures had inevitably emerged among former allies as some one-time activists were willing to accept the compromises the Pheu Thai party had been making with the establishment.

In the 2023 national election, the Move Forward Party, made up of former Future Forward candidates who lambasted the junta as well as some first-time candidates who had gained prominence during the 2020-2021 protests, with a platform that called for an end to military conscription and reform of lèse-majesté laws, did extraordinarily well. It did not win a majority of seats in Parliament, but it got a plurality, meaning that as the leading part of a coalition its leader should have been able to form a government. Netiwit was thrilled when Toto became a member of Parliament, even though it meant some of his closest collaborators had gone from spending most of their time on projects at the press to working with the Move Forward Party.

However, once again the monarchy, the military, and conservative elites stopped Move Forward's leader from becoming Prime Minister and forming a government. The civilian party that did second best in the election, Pheu Thai, *was* allowed to form a government, which was heralded by some, including some progressives, as a welcome step forward, as an end to the bad old days that began with the coup. But the price of power for Pheu Thai was agreeing to work with representatives of the junta and to stop pushing for some of the changes that it had called for while campaigning.

By the end of 2023, lèse-majesté reform was completely off the table. Not only that, but there was a new round of 112 prosecutions, with defamation of royals defined as loosely as it has ever been and carrying penalties as stiff as they have ever been. One person given a long jail sentence was Anon Nampa, who had been the first speaker at a 2020 protest to shift from playfulness to direct speech in criticizing the royal stifling of democracy.

Ending conscription was off the table as well by late 2023, no matter that Pheu Thai, the party of new Prime Minister Srettha Thavisin, had called for an end to the draft when campaigning. Prayuth was no longer head of the government, but he had gotten a new influential post in the administration, and so had members of the junta. Thailand was no longer under direct military rule, but it was not fully democratic either.

In April 2024, as the tenth anniversary of the coup neared, the hopeful spirit among young progressives epitomized by the giant 2020 protests and the May 2023 election results had been doused. There were some victories that progressives could celebrate. Pheu Thai, for example, had kept one of its promises and continued to support LGBTQ+ rights, putting Thailand on the path to become one of the rare countries in Asia where same-sex unions are legal. And even if there was a lot of continuity between the new government led by Srettha, a tycoon, and the one that had been led by Prayuth, a general, at least the country was back in the mode of expecting to have regular elections.

But soon after the tenth anniversary of the 2014 coup passed, the authorities showed just how keen they were on ensuring that Move Forward Party would have no further role in politics. The Constitutional Court had ordered the party to stop publicly campaigning to reform Section 112, and in a unanimous ruling all nine judges voted to dissolve the party. Eleven senior Move Forward Party executives were banned from politics for a decade, on top of at least forty-four members of parliament who were accused of violating Section 112, many of them for co-sponsoring a bill to amend that law.

Just as the banning of the Future Forward Party led to the creation of the Move Forward Party, now the banning of the

Move Forward Party has led to the creation of a People's Party. Some Move Forward members shifted immediately to align with this new organization. Krittapas and Mew, for example, became members and began working for the People's Party.

Most Thais, however, are no longer willing to protest, fatigued from 2020 and its aftermath. They have focused more on the country's stagnant economic prospects. Netiwit spends most of his time at Sam Yan Press, and he has opened a small beer bar and community space to complement the noodle restaurant. His local activities have been tolerated by authorities even as they continue to be a regime of repression. As of October 2024, nearly 2,000 people have been prosecuted under politically motivated lawsuits, ranging from infringing Section 112 to violations of the Public Assembly Act. Now no longer under the backdrop of constant protest, these cases are lost among Thailand's frenetic news cycle. Like Hong Kong, ensnaring large numbers of dissidents within the labyrinthine and opaque battleground of a politically charged legal system was a successful pivot; it gave authorities more freedom to act behind closed doors without the dramatic visuals and the opportunity for mass participation that had previously kept those protest movements alive.

Occasionally, however, grim reminders of the toll that incarceration has on these dissidents does make headlines. The use of lèse-majesté laws reached a newfound severity in January 2024 when the courts sentenced Mongkhon Thirakot, an activist and an online clothes vendor, to fifty years in jail, the longest sentence ever for 112 offenses, based on messages and posts on Facebook. And then there was the case of twenty-eight-year-old Netiporn "Bung" Sanesangkhom, one of the most visible members of a small monarchy-reform protest group that continued their activities long after the main movement had died down. Bung launched a hunger strike calling for reforms to the justice system and the release of fellow political detainees. After more than 100 days, prison officials announced that she had passed away after her heart "stopped suddenly." Prime Minister Srettha called for an investigation into Bung's death, but he was dismissed from office himself and replaced by another member of his party soon after.

Meanwhile, Wong is serving time in a prison in Hong Kong and awaiting further sentencing that will determine how many additional years he will have to spend incarcerated.

Netiwit, too, could well face the long arm of the law. Doubling down on his pacifism, early in 2024 he refused to participate in the draft lottery central to Thailand's conscription. Candidates assemble and draw cards, with a red card meaning they would have to serve in the military for two years and a black card meaning that they were exempt. It is grimly fitting that this ceremony resembles the selection of contestants in the *Hunger Games*.

Netiwit was ordered to appear in court this fall, but he successfully sought a deferral. He did not, though, let October 13 pass without posting a birthday greeting to Joshua Wong on X. Back in 2022, some Milk Tea Alliance members in Bangkok even bought ad space on the back of minicabs, known as *tuk tuks*, to carry posters of Wong's face that wished him a happy twenty-sixth birthday. Joshua was in prison then, as he is now, but he managed to ask a friend to convey his appreciation to the Thai activists who continued to support him. He singled one out by name: Netiwit.

Hong Kong

In the early 2010s, something remarkable happened in Hong Kong. A group of teenagers learned that local authorities planned to alter the way civics and history were taught in schools, and install a curriculum known as the "Moral and National Education" program.

Among other things, the teaching manual praised one-party rule, describing the Communist Party as an "advanced, selfless, and unified governing body," while criticizing the US two-party system as a "bitter inter-party conflict that harms the people." The program aimed to cultivate a "positive and optimistic attitude" among the children of Hong Kong.

The students, who were only fifteen or sixteen years old, were determined to avoid the type of intensely patriotic schooling that kids on the Chinese mainland were getting, which they described as "brainwashing."

It was extraordinary that the teenagers accurately foresaw that changing the curriculum went beyond education—it was part of a broader set of troubling moves that, if unchecked, would end up transforming Hong Kong into a place much like the cities across the border on the mainland.

In Hong Kong, they remained free to learn about the 1989 massacre near Tiananmen Square, including how troops had fired automatic weapons at unarmed civilians after weeks of non-violent student protests. Meanwhile, their peers across the border either received no lessons on the event or were taught that the People's Liberation Army and the People's Armed Police exercised great restraint and restored "order" to cities that had been thrown into "chaos" by "rioters" backed by nefarious "black hand" intellectuals and Westerners.

Public mourning ceremonies could still be held each June 4 in Hong Kong to honor the victims. Local newspapers could carry stories and bookstores could stock volumes about the events, including a second massacre in Chengdu. Students argued that if the curriculum was forced to align with mainland standards, it could pave the way for banning vigils for the martyrs and restricting what newspapers could publish and bookstores could sell.

The teenagers didn't want their younger siblings or future children to grow up learning only positive accounts of the Communist Party and to be unaware of events like the Great Chinese Famine, caused by Mao Zedong's Great Leap Forward industrial and agricultural policies, or the mass killings during the Cultural Revolution.

Democracy was of course much more restricted on the mainland than in Hong Kong, where some government posts were still filled through open elections. The rule of law was weaker on the mainland, where courts lacked independence.

According to the Basic Law, the quasi-constitution agreed upon by Beijing and London which took effect in 1997, Hong

Kong's way of life was supposed to be preserved for fifty years. The Basic Law guaranteed that the city would be able to maintain its distinctive ways until 2047. This agreement promised that Hong Kong people would eventually govern Hong Kong. Yet, it often seemed that the Chief Executive, influenced by or seeking approval from Beijing, was unwilling to honor this fifty-year grace period.

Although some seats in Hong Kong's parliamentary body, the Legislative Council, were elected, many were reserved for specific constituencies, ensuring a strong pro-Beijing bloc. While the Chief Executive was also "elected," only candidates approved by a Beijing-aligned nominating committee of fewer than 1,500 members were eligible to run.

Students argued that Hong Kong's distinct identity was about to be eroded, and they urged the public to resist these changes, just as they had opposed a proposed security law in 2003 that threatened freedom of speech and assembly. They founded an organization called Scholarism to push back against the curriculum. They began holding protests to convince not just their classmates but also adults to join them.

On one side, there was Leung Chun-ying, the city's pro-Beijing Chief Executive who had risen to power through a rigged election, and behind him there was the might of the Chinese Communist Party. On the other, there were determined young people armed with slogans, placards, and banners who relied on rallies and other non-violent civil disobedience tactics.

Key members of Scholarism included its two co-founders, Joshua Wong and Ivan Lam, and a young woman named Agnes Chow who joined the organization in 2012. In late August of that year, Scholarism staged a sit-in protest at Hong Kong's government headquarters, where Lam and some other members began a hunger strike, which lasted several days.

Remarkably, Scholarism's efforts succeeded. On September 8, C. Y. Leung announced a "temporary withdrawal" of the national education course.

Following this victory, Wong, Chow, and their peers continued to engage in uphill battles, including the 2014 Umbrella Movement. Unlike previous efforts to resist specific policies, the Umbrella Movement sought full democracy by changing the Chief Executive selection process. Initially led by two professors and an elderly preacher, the movement soon shifted to being led largely by high school students like Wong and Agnes Chow, along with university students like Nathan Law and Alex Chow. Their goal was to transform what was essentially a selection process into a genuine election.

For nearly eighty days, the Umbrella Movement established large occupation sites in Hong Kong's central business district. Dramatic clashes unfolded as riot police used pepper spray, tear gas, and batons to disperse protesters. Agnes Chow withdrew from the movement temporarily, citing pressure, online abuse, and concerns for her family's safety due to her involvement. However, she soon returned to the protests with renewed commitment.

In the end, the Umbrella Movement failed to achieve any of its demands, setting a pattern for later struggles that often concluded in either stalemates or with the authorities prevailing. But there were occasional triumphs. Wong, Agnes Chow, and Nathan Law founded a political party named Demosistō, a portmanteau derived from Greek for "people" and Latin for "to stand." The party fielded Law in the 2016 Legislative Council election, and, at twenty-three, he became the youngest candidate ever elected to the body.

Agnes Chow was set to continue her studies at Hong Kong's Baptist University when Law's term as a legislator was abruptly cut short. Prior to the election, the Electoral Affairs Commission introduced a new requirement for all candidates to sign a "confirmation form" during nomination, affirming their recognition that Hong Kong is an inseparable part of China, and six candidates had already been disqualified for refusing to sign. At the council's inaugural meeting, Law and other legislators modified the standard protocols of the oath-taking ceremony, a form of inserting a protest angle into an official ceremony that had become something of a tradition among candidates from opposition parties ever since 2004, when a newly elected pro-democracy lawmaker used the occasion to shout slogans.

The oath required council members to swear allegiance to the Hong Kong Special Administrative Region of the People's Republic of China. Nathan Law had given a speech before, and then took the oath as if "the People's Republic of China" was a question. The National People's Congress in Beijing intervened, mandating that the oath be taken "sincerely" and "solemnly." After months of litigation, six lawmakers were disqualified, including Law, who was thrown in jail a month later for his involvement in the 2014 Umbrella Movement.

Demosistō wanted to find someone to run for Law's now-vacant seat, and Chow was the clear choice. One poster created for her campaign brings together themes that later came to be associated with the Milk Tea Alliance. The poster was captioned "The Younger Games," and it showed Agnes Chow pulling back the string of a bow, about to shoot an arrow, and looking a lot like Jennifer Lawrence did in the *Hunger Games* films.

To qualify for office, Chow had to renounce her British citizenship, costing her a potential safety net if the government chose to prosecute her. This sacrifice proved futile when, in January 2018, she was barred from running.

In 2019, the Hong Kong government again courted controversy. Chief Executive Carrie Lam's administration attempted to push through an extradition bill that would have allowed the transfer of criminal suspects from Hong Kong to jurisdictions with which it had no formal extradition agreements, including mainland China, Taiwan, and Macau. This raised widespread fears that Hong Kong activists, journalists, and dissidents could be extradited to mainland China, where there was no due process in the legal system and the courts were controlled by the Communist Party. The bill undermined Hong Kong's judicial autonomy and posed a severe threat to freedom of speech and civil rights.

The bill's introduction sparked the "Be Water Revolution," the longest-lasting movement with the largest crowds in Hong Kong's history. The movement drew inspiration from Hong Kong martial artist Bruce Lee's philosophical advice to "be water." For the protesters, this meant adopting fluid, unpredictable tactics to evade and outmaneuver the police, creating a dynamic strategy that kept law enforcement on the back foot. The tactics inspired later protest movements in countries like Thailand and Burma and helped form the Milk Tea Alliance. In response, Hong Kong police escalated their use of force, conducting mass arrests

58 and shutting down public transit to prevent gatherings, while sealing off protest sites. Widespread accusations of police brutality emerged, with videos showing police tackling protesters and, in some cases, using live ammunition—actions that drew international criticism and fueled local outrage.

The movement has since been portrayed in official publications much like the Tiananmen protests: a narrative of "chaos" followed by the "restoration of order," casting the events as a black-and-white conflict between meddling "foreigners" and patriotic citizens.

"Be Water" was indeed more militant than earlier struggles, and saw more acts of violence by protesters than in Tiananmen. By the end, it adopted a do-or-die mentality, encapsulated in the phrase *lam chau*, which is the Cantonese equivalent of a *Hunger Games* slogan: "If we burn, you burn with us."

In fact, most participants engaged in non-violent civil disobedience. Many leaders criticized any acts of violence, and protesters only resorted to potentially harmful tactics after prolonged police brutality and unchecked attacks by thugs aligned with authorities. Additionally, the core demands of the protests evolved into a plea to protect the right to protest, with calls for an investigation into police conduct. Chief Executive Carrie Lam ignored these demands, refusing even to acknowledge the escalating police violence.

After months of protests, Lam finally withdrew the bill but refused to resign or initiate an investigation. In what was widely viewed as a referendum on the government, pro-democracy candidates won a landslide victory in local elections at the end of 2019.

In late 2020, Agnes Chow, along with Joshua Wong and Ivan Lam, were jailed for their involvement in protests outside the Hong Kong police headquarters during the "Be Water" movement. Chow received a ten-month sentence. Amnesty International criticized the ruling, saying that "authorities are sending a warning to anyone who dares openly criticize the government that they could be next."

During her time in jail, Chow spent her days reading and listening to the radio, saying she "always looked forward to getting letters." On Twitter, she shared that Wong was struggling with incarceration but appreciated the support he received from people outside.

Upon her release, Chow was met by supporters dressed in black and wearing yellow masks—a color symbolizing resistance to "mainlandization." She maintained a low public profile for over two years, reportedly due to the physical and psychological toll of her prison term. Hong Kong's most prominent activists have all faced either imprisonment, exile, or, in Chow's case, a precarious in-between state, not imprisoned but lacking true freedom, with the constant threat of renewed persecution hanging over her.

Effectively under house arrest by 2022, the authorities pressured Chow to remain silent, warning that speaking out could lead to re-imprisonment. During this time, even close friends found it difficult to stay in touch with her, and she feared repercussions against her family.

In late 2023, she agreed to take a "patriotic reeducation" trip just across the border in Shenzhen, where officials attempted to pressure her into renouncing her political beliefs. In exchange, they returned her passport. She is now working toward a master's degree at the University of Toronto.

In 2020, a controversy erupted over the Disney live action film *Mulan*. The lead actress had voiced support for the Hong Kong police during the 2019 protests, prompting calls for a boycott from Hong Kong protesters and international supporters, including Netiwit. Further criticism arose due to scenes having been filmed in Xinjiang while a massive network of forced indoctrination camps were in place. The closing credits thanked the Xinjiang authorities for their help. Some netizens, in supporting the boycott, suggested that there was a "real Mulan" who deserved to be celebrated: Agnes Chow.

Burma

When Tun Myint came to see me in my office hours in the early 1990s, I was an early-career professor of history at Indiana University. He told me that he was from Burma but had come to Bloomington from Bangkok, where he had lived as a refugee. He said he was a political science major interested in similarities and differences between the 1988 protests in his homeland and the 1989 ones in China.

It was my first encounter with someone from Burma, with anyone who had taken part in protests in Southeast Asia, and with political exile from any place that would eventually be associated with the Milk Tea Alliance. Until I met Tun Myint—who told me at our first meeting that he liked to be referred to simply as "Tun," though Burmese does not have the same standard division between first names and surnames as many languages have—the only political exiles I had met were Tiananmen activists from the Chinese mainland. Tun was also the first person I had ever met who had carried a rifle in the rain forest as a member of an armed guerrilla unit.

I did not know that meeting him would lead to me deciding some two decades later to take a trip to Burma when it seemed that Tun's country was finally democratizing. It helped set me on the path to writing this book, because my first conversations with him touched on potential parallels between East Asian and Southeast Asian youth movements.

Southeast Asia has a long tradition of student protests, and I had spent my graduate school years researching and writing a dissertation on Chinese youth movements. I also spent much of my first years as a professor working on the Tiananmen protests. As natural as it might seem for someone like me to have paid attention to Southeast Asian activism, including the Bangkok demonstrations and massacre of 1976, the Burmese events of 1988, and the People Power Movement in the Philippines in between, I had only a passing knowledge of those events. East Asian Studies and Southeast Asian Studies were, and still often are, considered distinctively different fields. Burma, Thailand, and the Philippines were as off the map in my training as Cuba and Chile.

Meeting Tun changed my perspectives. He explained that he wanted to place what in Burma is called "8888"—a name derived from a key protest taking place on the eighth day of the eight month of 1988—into comparative perspective. The natural place to look for connections was in other parts of Asia.

Tun saw the Tiananmen protests as similar in basic ways to the Burmese struggle of 1988. Young protesters had played leading roles in both, and sometimes paid for their activism with their lives. He had seen soldiers kill not just students but unarmed civilians from all walks of life in the streets of Yangon, his nation's capital, in the summer and fall of 1988. He knew that there were many people living in a capital city far to the north, Beijing, who saw similar things happen there less than twelve months later.

Americans all seemed to know at least a bit about what had happened in Beijing in 1989. They often had no idea that anything special had happened in Yangon in 1988, even though Tun was sure—and he is right—that soldiers had killed more people in Burma than in China.

Tun had spent months on the Thai-Burmese border in an area where soldiers of the ruling junta and armed guerrillas were fighting skirmishes. I nodded, thinking that it must have been worryingly dangerous to try to stay safe when two sides were clashing like that around you.

"I was one of the guerrillas," he said.

Tun was born in a village outside of Yangon that lacked regular supplies of running water and electricity, and he spent his childhood in the 1970s there. No one of the generation before his in his family had finished high school, let alone gone to a university. He was one of six brothers in a farming family.

Tun describes his father as someone who had a reputation locally for being an outspoken critic of the corrupt and oppressive practices of the junta who had taken control of Burma in a 1962 coup. Tun's father did not join any opposition group or take part in a major protest, but his sons grew up knowing about the distaste he felt for the military.

Prior to the coup, the country had seemed as though it might end up one of Southeast Asia's great success stories, not one of its great tragedies. In the nineteenth century, the British conquered this region of Asia and created what we now know as Burma. This new entity was patched together out of an old Burmese kingdom and lands surrounding it that had populations of varied ethnicities and had often been completely independent from that kingdom. Independence activists and revolutionaries were plotting to end British rule when Japanese forces occupied the country during World War II. The leader of the army and thus the most powerful of these revolutionaries, Aung San, became the minister of war in the Japanese puppet state, but as the Allies advanced on Burma, he switched sides and drove the Japanese forces out, and began negotiating with the British for autonomy. Aung San was assassinated along with most of his cabinet six months before Burma declared independence in 1948.

There were signs of trouble from the start. Burma was plagued by ideological and ethnic divisions left over from tensions between pre-colonial kingdoms. Many of the non-Bamar (that is, Burmese) ethnic groups such as the Shan and the Karen engaged in guerrilla warfare to fight for their own states, and in response General Ne Win staged a coup and took over the country in 1962.

By the time Tun entered his teenage years and began his political awakening, the early promise of the nation had become a distant memory. The military did not just hold political power; the economy was in a terrible state. Ne Win had proclaimed his desire to transform Burma into a special sort of socialist country, and promised to divide the wealth among the people. The reality, however, was that Burma had become a place in which the military ran everything, operating as an elite class above all others. The only way for anyone to get ahead was to be part of it or collaborate with it.

Tun's road toward activism began in the teshops of Yangon, which were crucial hubs for cultural and political exchanges. As a high schooler in the mid-1980s, Tun began to hang out in them for hours on end, drinking a sweet version of tea with dairy in it. He and others would share grievances and swap dreams. Ne Win's nearly three decades of autocratic rule had driven the country into the ground. The regime wiped out the savings of millions of people overnight when it imposed two rounds of currency demonetization, declaring that certain denominations of bills were immediately invalid. The United Nations gave Burma "Least Developed Country" status in 1987.

In 1988, police refusal to discipline a government official's relative for brawling with university students provoked a series of demonstrations that would escalate into hundreds of thousands of people—including Tun and many of his tea shop friends—gathering in the streets on August 8, 1988, calling for democracy, economic reforms, and an end to military rule. The movement was known as the 8888 Uprising, and large protests continued in Yangon for about a month. Demonstrations and general strikes also emerged in Pyay, Taungoo, Mandalay, and Mawlamyine. The junta declared martial law on September 18, and ordered security forces to fire into crowds and to conduct mass arrests. The most-frequently cited estimate is 3,000 killed, but the total is likely significantly higher.

"I saw the shooting in front of me," Tun told Minnesota Public Radio years later. "Some of my own colleagues in the strike were shot and some of them died. That visionary evidence that I saw was a call to me that I must fight this government by armed struggle." He was just eighteen.

"I just wanted to establish a student army and join it. That was it," Tun told me. "I did not know any groups, and it was a blind decision to go to the border area and organize an armed revolution." He ended up in the Three Pagoda Pass area on the border with Thailand, and stayed in the rain forest until 1990. When some elders offered to help him cross the border, he took the chance, traveling to Bangkok and becoming a refugee. There, he taught himself English. With support from the US Embassy and the United Nations High Commissioner for Refugees, he received a scholarship and, in 1993, arrived at Indiana University.

It was during the 8888 Uprising that Aung San's daughter, Aung San Suu Kyi, emerged as a symbol to rally around, when she addressed half a million protesters in front of Yangon's revered Shwedagon Pagoda. Tun was among the massive crowd that day, hearing her call for a non-violent movement to topple the military. "Like most people," he told me, "I applauded her remarks." Her speech gave him hope, framing the movement as a "second struggle for independence"—the first being from British colonial rule, led by her father, and the second from dictatorship. He thought this would unite people across Burma's ethnic groups in a shared desire to end tyranny.

But soon after, Suu Kyi was placed under house arrest and separated from her husband and children, who lived in England. (She would spend fifteen out of the next twenty-one years in confinement.) When the junta gave in to pressure and allowed general elections to take place in 1990, her party, the National League for Democracy (NLD), won four out of every five seats in parliament, but the military refused to acknowledge the results.

Her sons accepted the Nobel Peace Prize on her behalf a year later.

It would be another quarter of a century before Suu Kyi and the NLD won the right to openly contest in another general election. (They had won 43 out of 45 vacant seats in by-elections in 2012, when she became a member of parliament for the first time.) The result was a landslide victory for the NLD, and Suu Kyi was appointed State Counselor, a position created especially for her, in effect making her the Prime Minister of Burma.

But the NLD's track record in power disappointed many ethnic minority communities. The national party failed to devolve power to regional and ethnic-minority state governments. Under the 2008 constitution, the ruling party appoints state- and regional-level ministers, and the NLD frequently handpicked favorites even in the face of legislative majorities or pluralities held by other parties. Suu Kyi did little to constrain the military in fighting against Kachin and Shan minorities, and made little progress in negotiations to end decades-long civil wars. Her government even called on the military to suppress an ethnic Rakhine insurgent group.*

Tun and many other activists felt that Suu Kyi was irredeemably tainted by what she did as the State Counselor of Burma, when she worked with the military authorities, purged Muslim candidates from her party's electoral roles, and defended official policies that targeted the Rohingya minority for expulsion from Burma. She is seen as having been party to grotesque violations of human rights against the largely

*For background, see the Crisis Group report available here: https://www.crisisgroup.org/asia/south-east-asia/myanmar/307-avoidable-war-politics-and-armed-conflict-myanmars-rakhine-state

Muslim ethnic group, policies that have been widely criticized as genocidal.

Many were further disillusioned by the positive stance she took toward the Chinese Communist Party, when she was willing to meet with its leaders in her capacity as part of the government. She refused to speak out against Beijing's human rights abuses in Xinjiang, where more than a million Uyghurs and other Muslim minorities have been incarcerated in massive forced-labor and concentration camps. While China's actions in Xinjiang have received more attention recently, Tibetans continue to suffer severe human rights abuses and "cultural genocide." These include the imprisonment of political dissidents, suppression of Tibetan culture and religious practices, and the forced separation of a million Tibetan children from their families to attend mandatory boarding schools that teach only Mandarin and promote ideological indoctrination.

If the anti-junta movement is associated with the Milk Tea Alliance, as it sometimes is, linking it to Suu Kyi becomes challenging. Hong Kong exiles increasingly see their struggle as similar to that of Tibetans and Uyghurs, as distinct cultures on the fringes of China that Beijing is forcing to conform. For the NLD to be associated with actions against the Rohingya and for its leaders to pose with officials involved in Beijing's persecution of ethnic groups in Western China positions the party against, rather than aligned with, the Milk Tea Alliance.

Reflecting on the 2021 "people's revolutionary war," Tun sees it as validation of the decision he made in 1988. Tun finds inspiration in the slogans of a new generation of activists, such as, "If you won't let us dream, we won't let you sleep," which accompanies the pot-banging protests disrupting city life and awakening people from complacency. This resonates with the outrage he felt as a high school student, and he understands why young people are again taking up arms.

When the 8888 Uprising changed Tun's life, Ye Myint Win, not yet known as Nickey Diamond, was a five-year-old boy living in Mandalay. He remembers getting his first whiff of tear gas and hearing gunshots when the junta moved against the protesters. He later heard stories from aunts and uncles who had joined them.

Diamond's family sold mangoes, and they were not part of the Buddhist majority. They were Muslims.* He was not particularly politically minded as a child, Diamond says, but he did have a sense from early in life that he lived in a troubled land without an effective government, and he was aware that he belonged to a group that is often discrimination against in Burma.

Diamond's political awareness grew when in his teens he met a Mormon couple who were on their mission in Mandalay. He remembers the couple fondly, though he notes with some pride that while they influenced his view of the world they never succeeded in converting him. The couple had him read *The 7 Habits of Highly Effective People* to improve his English,

---

*Many foreigners associate anti-Muslim discrimination in Burma solely with the Rohingya, whom the government labels "Bengalis" and treats as outsiders, despite their longstanding roots in the country. However, discrimination also impacts other Muslim groups, including Bamar Muslims and Muslim members of recognized ethnic groups. At a public event, Nickey corrected a moderator's assumption that he was Rohingya, clarifying that he is a "Burmese Muslim," specifically a Bamar from a Muslim family.

and they were the ones who dubbed him "Nickey." Later, he took "Diamond" as his last name since that is the English translation of one of the words in his father's name.

He became a determined and eclectic reader, no thanks to Burma's education system, which had been decimated by the junta's policies. If you were a member of the elite, you might be able to go to an international school or study abroad and get a real education. That was impossible for most Burmese, and doubly so for members of ethnic groups like the Rohingya, Shan, Kachin, Rakhine, Karenni, Chin, and Karen. Diamond had to educate himself, and he frequented libraries, reading whatever he could get his hands on and working on his English. He read *Nineteen Eighty-Four*, *Animal Farm*, and *The Old Man and the Sea*, which he still finds inspiring, due to the main character's determination to persevere. He read a biography of Martin Luther King Jr., and describes Hannah Arendt as his "current intellectual hero."

After finishing high school, Diamond discovered that he would not be granted the full citizenship status that most Bamar get automatically when they turn eighteen. Even though his parents and grandparents were all Burmese citizens, he was told he would have to wait eight years to get his citizenship papers and be able to travel, but a bribe would speed things along. The idea disgusted him and he refused. It was a trigger that made him determined to fight a rotten system, and he began volunteering for various activist groups. He was also incredibly inspired by Aung San Suu Kyi, and he read everything by her. But like many other activists, his views on The Lady began to change. He found it increasingly hard to admire someone who was working with the military. By the 2010s, he went from someone who had doubts about her to viewing her as hypocritical, because it became clear that she did not view Muslims in Burma as part of "the people" who deserved her concern. She was complicit in the treatment of the Rohingya and was committed to "Burmanizing" the country.

In 2019, the NLD and the military began erecting statues of Aung San Suu Kyi's father all around the country. Aung San had long been seen as the "Father of the Nation," and he had called for the creation of Burma in which regions viewed as homelands by non-Bamar ethnic groups would have a great deal of autonomy via a federal system of governance. This vision of the father was tarnished by his daughter's apparent lack of interest in pushing for the sort of federalist vision of the country he had embraced. "Karenni people highly respect General Aung San," Nickey told *Al Jazeera*, but they have been persecuted for decades. Since Burma gained its independence, he said, "Burman politicians and the military leaders failed to keep Aung San's promises of federalism. As a result, minority ethnic people interpreted the erection of the statue as part of Burmanisation."

In 2007, Burma was rocked by the biggest wave of protests since 1988. Called the Saffron Revolution in reference to the color of the robes of the tens of thousands of Buddhist monks who participated and took center stage, this movement arose in response to the abrupt end of vital subsidies, which sent fuel prices skyrocketing. When the military refused to apologize for violently suppressing a demonstration and injuring three monks, Buddhists across the country declared *thabeik hmauk*, or the overturning of alms bowls, and refused to accept donations from regime officials, preventing them from accumulating merit for reincarnation. An estimated 150,000 people, including between 30,000 and 50,000 monks, marched through the streets of Yangon on September 24 to protest a military crackdown that featured not just the usual arrests, killings, and disappearances, but also systematic raids on monasteries.

Diamond was among the young activists in Mandalay who staged related demonstrations. He and his friends always covered their faces with masks, and were worried about reprisals from the soldier and police.

Diamond escaped arrest, but the Saffron Revolution was a turning point for him. He founded Youth for Social Change Myanmar to encourage young people to express themselves not through protests, but through self-education, along the path that he himself followed. The emails he exchanged with others in the group were filled with suggestions of things to read and programs to join. Diamond shared information about short camps in other parts of Southeast Asia where like-minded young people could learn about peacebuilding. Some of these camps were funded by the Open Society, while others were led by members of the Engaged Buddhism Movement, including by people who had worked with Netiwit's mentor Sulak Sivaraksa.

In 2013, Diamond received a Norwegian government scholarship to pursue a master's in human rights at Mahidol University in Bangkok. His thesis focused on "violence and recovery" in Burma, and he also began documenting the abuse of the Rohingya in Rakhine state. As he was earning his degree, he spent six years in Yangon as a Human Rights Specialist with Fortify Rights, a prominent organization highlighting the Burmese military's abuses to an international audience, often aiming to spur a response—a practice that has drawn some criticism for alleged sensationalism in certain cases.

It was during this time that Nickey Diamond drew the ire of the military regime for his outspokenness and willingness to talk to the press. He told me that he was followed every day by police and members of military intelligence who would sometimes wait for him outside of his apartment. They would also follow his wife when she went grocery shopping and ran errands.

In late 2020, Aung San Suu Kyi and the NLD again won a general election in a landslide. This time, the army claimed the results were fraudulent, and overthrew the government again before the parliament members could convene. The junta, now under the control of General Min Aung Hlaing, once again arrested Aung San Suu Kyi, who was later sentenced to four years in prison.

Then the Spring Revolution erupted nationwide, with the three-finger salute becoming a prominent protest symbol, while netizens joined the Milk Tea Alliance's online movements. Independent monitoring groups report that nearly 6,000 civilians have been killed and over 27,000 have been arrested. The military crackdown prompted armed resistance and so far, the intense fighting has resulted in an estimated 50,000 to more than 70,000 deaths and the United Nations reported that over 3 million people have been displaced.

For Diamond, it became clear that staying inside the country would mean risking not only his own life but those of his wife and their young children. His wife, who ran a business that helped poor farmers get better prices for their goods, also angered the government for refusing to pay a form of extortion that would have allowed her to keep operating. The authorities shut down the company and seized their assets.

For weeks after the coup, the military conducted house-to-house searches looking for dissidents. Diamond and his family were warned, and hid in a safe house in Yangon, before fleeing to an area on the Thai-Burma border than was under the control of the Karen ethnic group, who sheltered them. Diamond refers to the region as the "liberated" part of the country, but they were still targets of bombing raids against civilian areas. They crossed the border into Thailand, and eventually made their way as refugees to Germany, where they have been living since.

He has stayed linked to Fortify Rights, serving on its board of governance. As part of his focus on using international legal procedures to try to punish or at least shame the Burmese authorities, he and fifteen others filed a criminal complaint against senior military leaders with the Federal Public Prosecutor General of Germany under the principle of universal jurisdiction in January 2023. The complaint alleged war crimes and crimes against humanity committed in the military's brutal operations in Rakhine State in 2016 and 2017 as well as in the wake of the 2021 coup. However, the German prosecutor dismissed the case, citing the absence of the accused in Germany and doubt about how the case would be distinct from similar ones in other international fora. In addition to his involvement in legal actions, Diamond takes any opportunity he can to appear on panels. In these talks he refers to an ongoing genocide targeting the Rohingya. He does this keeping his voice calm, but wearing a black shirt emblazoned with his favorite painting, Edvard Munch's *The Scream*.

I first met Nickey Diamond in May 2023 in a lakeside harbor district not far from the University of Konstanz, where he was working on a doctorate on forms of anti-Muslim hate speech in Burma. When we found a suitable café, I offered to buy him a drink. Perhaps some kind of milk tea beverage, I suggested? He opted for juice, and I chuckled. I had spent more than a year meeting up with people connected to Milk Tea Alliance movements, and not one of them had wanted milk tea. Cappuccinos, yes. Lattes, yes. Soft drinks and smoothies, yes. But no milk tea.

Diamond understood why I found this amusing, but he stressed to me that he does not really think of himself as part of the Milk Tea Alliance. Or, at least, ties to it are not central to his identity as an activist or as a scholar. It is true that he studied in Thailand, but he feels that for his own work, paying attention to the problems in multiple parts of Burma and keeping up with trends across that country is a big enough job. He does note, though, that many of his Burmese and Thai colleagues who are more focused on general human rights issues than on anti-Muslim hate speech and discrimination per se, as he tends to be, take a wider view, keeping up more than he does with, for example, Hong Kong events. He also appreciates that Fortify Rights, while especially linked to Burma, is an organization that emphasizes connections between struggles in different regions and is seen as a stalwart of the Milk Tea Alliance. The non-profit has close ties to a cultural center in Bangkok called The Fort, which often hosts the same events as the bar run by Netiwit and the Sam Yan Press, including a film criticizing Beijing's human rights abuses in Xinjiang, with the same Uyghur activists in exile speaking at both events.

Diamond told me that he was concerned about the rise of China, the "bad neighbor" to Burma, and he saw parallels between the way Beijing treated the Uyghurs and the way the Burmese junta treated the Rohingya. His focus, however, was on influencing international opinion, especially in Europe, and using international legal mechanisms to make the junta feel that there were costs to its policies.

To bring Western pressure on the junta, he felt, the key was in making political leaders outside of Asia more aware and more outraged about the situation in his homeland. To do that, it was often most effective to bring up parallels to Nazi anti-Semitism and the Holocaust. This was the best way to make clear that he felt there was one word that best characterized the treatment of the Rohingya: genocide.

Beginnings

Writing a book on the Milk Tea Alliance has led me to revisit familiar spots with new sets of questions to ponder, new people to meet, and a newfound interest in sites with historical resonances that I had not been aware of before. Like Tokyo's Hibiya Park, which had been a popular meeting place for exiles from different parts of Asia in the time of Sun Yat-sen, the Chinese revolutionary leader and the founding father of the Republic of China, known for his role in overthrowing the Qing Dynasty and promoting modern democratic ideas in early-twentieth-century China.

The park contained an exhibit devoted to Sun's deep friendship with Shokichi Umeya, a Tokyo businessman and early film impresario. Umeya was a supporter of political causes and part of a family that still owns the only restaurant right in the park, Hibiya Matsumotoro. The exhibit, which is in that restaurant, includes photographs and objects associated with the time Sun spent in Tokyo. Hibiya Matsumotoro held personal significance for Sun, especially in his courtship of Soong

Ch'ing-ling (Song Qingling), a prominent political figure, revolutionary, and advocate for women's rights who became his wife and was known as Madame Sun Yat-sen. Tokyo attracted many exiles from China and other parts of Asia. It was also a place where Japanese people, inspired by the Chinese revolutionary and eager for change, offered him not only friendship but financial support.

Sun was also intrigued by the experiences of Philippine insurgents, some of whom passed through Tokyo as exiles. A statue of the prominent Philippine revolutionary Jose Rizal stands in the park near Hibiya Matsumotoro. Although Rizal's time in Japan, including a stay near the park, was before Sun's, Sun did meet and collaborated closely with other Filipinos in Tokyo who shared Rizal's mission to free the Philippines from foreign control.

Another figure who greatly influenced Sun, especially in the early stages of his revolutionary thinking, was Liang Qichao, a pioneering advocate for reform whose ideas on reconstructing China's political and educational systems, as well as his emphasis on national strength, inspired Sun and others in the independence movement.

Liang is not a household name in most parts of the world, but over a century ago, he was widely considered China's leading intellectual. He was among the radicals who briefly gained the support of the Guangxu Emperor. In 1898, in what became known as the Hundred Days' Reform, the twenty-five-year-old Liang and his colleagues and the twenty-seven-year-old emperor set out to transform the Qing Empire in a manner similar to Japan's Meiji Restoration, envisioning a constitutional monarchy with modernized educational and bureaucratic institutions influenced by Western Europe.

The Hundred Days' Reform was so named because it was abruptly crushed by a palace coup led by Empress Dowager Cixi, who placed the young emperor under house arrest and reversed many of the policies. Some progressives were executed, and others, including Liang, were forced into exile. Liang went to the Japanese city of Yokohama, where he founded journals that published everything from original political fiction to essays and translations of works of history and social theory from all parts of the world, displaying a level of eclecticism comparable to the corpus that Netiwit and his Sam Yan colleagues have been creating for a different era.

During his first years in exile, Liang formed and broke alliances with other exiled Chinese reformers and even some revolutionaries, such as Sun. He closely followed events in other parts of Asia, seeking strategies that could help reform China, and maintained contact with progressives from various regions passing through Yokohama and nearby Tokyo.

Liang's omnivorous reading habits remind me of Netiwit, but I have also been struck by the parallels between Liang's life and that of Nathan Law, especially considering how much they both experienced before turning thirty.

Law rose to prominence at the age of twenty-one when he became a leader in the Umbrella Movement alongside Joshua Wong and Agnes Chow, and he was only twenty-three when he won a seat in the Legislative Council and was ousted from the body after protesting the oath-taking ceremony. In 2020, facing the newly imposed National Security Law, which criminalized dissent against the Chinese government, Law went into self-imposed exile to avoid arrest. Now based in London, he strives to find ways to draw international attention to the erosion of freedoms in the city he reluctantly left behind.

When I visited him in London in April of 2023, we talked about his efforts to link up with fellow exiles from Hong Kong and to learn from veterans of democracy movements all over Asia. It occurred to me that Liang could have been part of similar conversations more than a hundred years ago.

I have also thought a lot about the early twentieth-century activists profiled by Tim Harper in his magnum opus *Underground Asia: Global Revolutionaries and the Assault on Empire*. Some of these figures, like Liang and Sun Yat-sen, remain well-known. Others are largely forgotten, such as a Vietnamese would-be assassin who attempted to kill a French colonial official in southern China and was later buried as a hero in a cemetery for Chinese revolutionary martyrs. The ideologies they embraced—ranging from socialism and anarchism to Marxism-Leninism—distinguish them from most Milk Tea Alliance members, as do their tactics, which included targeted assassinations. Yet echoes of the Milk Tea Alliance can be seen in Harper's depiction of activists who shifted between local and transnational issues, forged bonds across borders, and shared a kinship while fighting against similarly oppressive regimes.

Sun Yat-sen may not resemble the activists of today's Milk Tea Alliance, yet, like them, he devoted his life to a long, multi-staged struggle that included both triumphant moments and significant setbacks. In his early years, he led a series of failed uprisings against the Qing Dynasty, before briefly serving as the Provisional President of the Republic of China in 1912—a position he soon lost to a military strongman. Though Sun was not a Marxist, he was a socialist and a patriot who spent his final years leading an anti-warlord, anti-imperialist alliance between the Nationalist Party he founded and the newly established Chinese Communist Party. His legacy is unique: revered by both Chiang Kai-shek's government in Taiwan and Mao Zedong's government in Beijing, he became a symbol of unity across political divides.

Yet, when he died, it was far from certain that either party would succeed in taking control of the Chinese mainland.

The Nationalists achieved the feat in 1928. The Communists took over two decades later, and the People's Republic of China was founded in 1949.

FURTHER READING

Introduction

This book covers the decade of youth protests from 2014 to 2024. Vince Bevins's *If We Burn: The Mass Protest Decade and the Missing Revolution* (Public Affairs, 2023) also examines protests but focuses on 2010 to 2020, including a key chapter on Hong Kong. Due to his focus on other regions like North Africa and Brazil, Bevins does not cover Thailand or Burma. Another recent work on past and present protests, with insights into youth activism in movements like Black Lives Matter, is Gal Beckerman's *The Quiet Before: On the Unexpected Origins of Radical Ideas* (Crown, 2022). My first mention of ties between Netiwit and Joshua Wong was in an essay, "Protesters of the World, Unite," for *Public Books* (March 15, 2023), which highlights Beckerman's insights. Other recent notable works on transnational activism include Tim Harper's *Underground Asia: Global Revolutionaries and the Assault on Empire* (Allen Lane, 2019); *The Anti-Colonial Transnational* (Cambridge, 2023), edited by Erez Manela and Heather Streets-Salter; Timothy Garton Ash's *Homelands: A Personal History of Europe* (Yale, 2023); and Micah Alpaugh's *Friends of Freedom: The Rise of Social Movements in the Age of Atlantic Revolutions* (Cambridge, 2021).

For background on youth struggles in Asia before the Milk Tea Alliance, *Student Activism in Asia: Between Protest and Powerlessness* (University of Minnesota Press, 2012), edited by Edward Aspinall and Meredith Weiss, is a solid starting point. Books covering protests in multiple Asian settings over the past decade are rare, but two notable works are Ming-Sho Ho's *Challenging Beijing's Mandate of Heaven: Taiwan's Sunflower*

Movement and Hong Kong's Umbrella Movement (Temple University Press, 2019), and *Sunflowers and Umbrellas: Social Movements, Expressive Practices, and Political Culture in Taiwan and Hong Kong* (Institute for East Asian Studies [Berkeley], 2020), edited by Thomas Gold and Sebastian Veg.

While the Milk Tea Alliance has not yet inspired book-length studies, several shorter works provide valuable insights. Some focus on the digital-era movements' similarities and differences from earlier ones, though not directly related to my primary interests here. Among articles covering multiple locations, I found the following particularly helpful: Fanny Potkin and Patpicha Tanakasempipat's "Power in Solidarity: Myanmar Protesters Inspired by Hong Kong and Thailand" (*Reuters*, February 9, 2021); Feliz Solomon and Wilawan Watcharasakwet's "Thailand's Protests Shift Tactics, Influenced by Hong Kong" (*Wall Street Journal*, October 18, 2020); Timothy McLaughlin's "How Milk Tea Became an Anti-China Symbol" (*The Atlantic*, October 13, 2020); and Mary Hui's "Hong Kong Crowdsourced a Protest Manual—And Myanmar's Already Using It" (*Quartz*, February 25, 2021).

I highly recommend a poignant BBC video by Tessa Wong, titled "Milk Tea Alliance: Thai and Hong Kong Activists on Fight for Democracy" (released November 7, 2020), which features a conversation between Hong Kong's Joshua Wong, shortly before his imprisonment, and sixteen-year-old Thai activist Akkarasorn Opilan. Filmed separately in Hong Kong and Bangkok, the video captures their mutual respect in a moving way.

Notable early scholarly works on the Milk Tea Alliance include Adam Dedman and Autumn Lai's "Digitally Dismantling

Asian Authoritarianism: Activist Reflections from the #MilkTeaAlliance" (*Contention*, 2021); Roger Lee Huang and Svetanant Chavalin's chapter on digital authoritarianism in *Activism and Authoritarian Governance in Asia* (Routledge, 2022); and Austin Wang and Adrian Rauchfleisch's "Understanding the #Milk Tea Alliance" in *Essays on China and U.S. Policy* (Wilson Center, 2022), available for free at the Wilson Center website. Another significant work is Wolfram Schaffar and Wongratanawin Praphakorn's article in the *Austrian Journal of South-East Asian Studies* (2021). A recent, concise assessment of the Milk Tea Alliance is provided by Thai scholars Tuwanont Phattharathanasut and Wichuta Teeeranabodee in "The Fourth Year of the Milk Tea Alliance," *E-International Relations* (April 8, 2024).

A relevant work worth noting, curiously titled with English terms but written in German, is Christine Knödler and Benjamin Knödler's *Young Rebels: 25 Jugendliche, Die Die Welt Verändern* (Hanser, 2020). It profiles some of the world's most famous young activists, such as Malala Yousafzai and Greta Thunberg. Joshua Wong has a chapter in the book, but most relevant here is that Netiwit does as well. Aimed at young readers, each chapter is brief and paired with a page showing repeated images symbolizing each activist's work—megaphones for Greta's speeches, umbrellas for Joshua Wong, and books for Netiwit.

The International Institute for Social History, with special holdings on the 2019 Hong Kong protests, Thailand's 2020 demonstrations, and earlier events in Thailand and Burma, deserves mention here. My visit to Amsterdam to review these materials—easily accessible through an online catalog and with assistance from helpful staff—was invaluable. Seeing various items side by side, from postcards depicting activists' hand gestures to magazine covers of crowds and a black umbrella from a 2020 Bangkok protest symbolizing both 1930s Thai events and recent Hong Kong protests, highlighted how symbols and strategies have circulated across East and Southeast Asia.

Thailand

For an overview of Thailand, *A History of Thailand: Fourth Edition* by Chris Baker and Pasuk Phongpaichit (2022) is a good starting point, particularly as this edition includes a brief discussion of the 2020 protests. On the history of youth protests in Thailand, the chapter by Prajak Kongkirati in the *Student Activism in Asia* volume, mentioned earlier, is valuable—even though it was published in 2012 and suggests that universities might no longer serve as hubs of activism, highlighting how student movements can evolve in unexpected ways. A powerful work on the Thammasat massacre, which is central to Thailand's activist history and relevant to Netiwit's life despite occurring before his birth, is Thongchai Winichakul's *Moments of Silence: The Unforgetting of the October 6, 1976, Massacre in Bangkok* (2020). Another noteworthy work on Cold War–era student activism and its legacy is *The Rise of the Octobrists in Contemporary Thailand* (2016) by Kanokrat Lertchoosakul, who has since published key articles on recent events, such as "The White Ribbon Movement: High School Students in the 2020 Thai Youth Protests" (*Critical Asian Studies*, 2021) and "The May 2023 Elections and the Triumph of Thai Youth Social Movements"(*Critical Asian Studies*, 2023), available on the publication's Commentary Board.

There is limited information on Netiwit's activities and views available in English. Unlike his mentor Sulak Sivaraksa, whose memoir *Loyalty Demands Dissent: Autobiography of an Engaged Buddhist* (1998) is in English, Netiwit's story is accessible only in Thai. His memoir, *Kansueksa Khong Nisit Leo: 5 Pi Nai Rua Chula* (*The Education of a Bad Student: A Memoir*), has multiple editions published by Sam Yan Press, the latest in 2022 with a foreword by Rung, who played a key role in the 2020 protests.

An early scholarly article featuring Netiwit is Penchan Phoborisut's "Contesting Big Brother: Joshua Wong, Protests, and the Student Network of Resistance in Thailand" (*International Journal of Communication*, 2019). Netiwit also appears in some general essays on the Milk Tea Alliance. An early English-language profile of him is Feliz Solomon's "Meet the Youthful Face of Resistance to Thailand's Junta" (*TIME*, June 28, 2017). Two notable interviews with him are available: one by Eraldo Souza Dos Santos for *New Bloom* (July 31, 2021), focusing on his interest in global social movements, titled "I Think We Can Learn a Lot from Black Thinkers: An Interview with Netiwit Chotiphatphaisal"; the other, emphasizing his religious views, is "The Monk and the Military" (*Tricycle: The Buddhist Review*, April 13, 2023).

For an in-depth look at the twists and turns of Thai politics over recent decades, the following books are key resources in English, addressing issues from elections and party bans to lèse-majesté prosecutions and defenses: Tyrell Haberkorn's *Dictatorship on Trial: Coups and the Future of Justice in Thailand* (Stanford, 2024) and Duncan McCargo and Anyarat Chattharakul's *Future Forward: The Rise and Fall of a Thai*

Political Party (NIAS Press, 2020). Two edited volumes by Pavin Chachavalpongpun are also notable: *Coup, King, Crisis: A Critical Interregnum in Thailand* (Yale Southeast Council, 2020) and *Rama X: The Thai Monarchy under King Vajiralongkorn* (Yale Southeast Asian Studies, 2023), each featuring works by prominent scholars, such as Claudio Sopranzetti. Additionally, Joshua Kurlantzick's commentaries for the Council of Foreign Relations offer valuable context, often situating Thai events alongside developments in neighboring countries, such as in his article "The State of Democracy in Southeast Asia is Bad and Getting Worse," *World Politics Review*, August 9, 2023.

To understand Bangkok events, I relied heavily on careful work by talented journalists and photographers who are based in the city during pivotal moments in the last decade. Photojournalist Cory Wright caught my attention with his "Scenes from Thailand's Massive Protests Demanding Reforms," *The Diplomat*, September 21, 2020. Bylines I learned to watch for, knowing I could depend on them, included Panu Wongcha-um (*Reuters*), Gwen Robinson (*Nikkei Asia*), Hannah Beech (*The New York Times*), Lisa Martin (*AFP*), Patpicha Tanakasempipat (*Bloomberg*), and Rebecca Ratcliffe (*The Guardian*).

Hong Kong

For a comprehensive discussion of additional resources on many topics mentioned in this chapter, refer to the "Further Readings" section of my earlier book, *Vigil: Hong Kong on the Brink* (Columbia Global Reports, 2020). The publications and films listed there, along with the book's notes, provide details about Agnes Chow (featured in documentaries by Matthew Torne and Joe Piscatella) and other individuals discussed here, including Chow's peers and older figures like Benny Tai (now imprisoned in Hong Kong) and Chan Kin-man and Reverend Chiu Yiu-ming (both now exiled in Taiwan), collectively noted here as the founders of the initial Occupy Central plan.

Below, I will limit my recommendations to English-language books published since I completed *Vigil* in November 2019, excluding notable news articles (such as those from *Hong Kong Free Press*), journal articles, think tank reports, and books in other languages—though valuable works on Hong Kong protests and repression exist in Chinese, Japanese, and several European languages, including Italian.

For in-depth discussions of the mid-to-late 2010s protests and the recent wave of repression, consider the following English-language books published in the last four years: Antony Dapiran's *City on Fire: The Fight for Hong Kong* (Scribe, 2020); Hana Meihan Davis's *For the Love of Hong Kong: A Memoir from My City Under Siege* (Global Dispatches, 2021); Michael C. Davis's *Freedom Undone: The Assault on Liberal Values and Institutions in Hong Kong* (Association for Asian Studies, 2024); Joshua Wong's *Unfree Speech: The Threat to Global Democracy and Why We Must Act Now*, translated by Jason Y. Ng (WH Allen, 2020); Nathan Law and Evan Fowler's *Freedom: How We Lose It and How We Fight Back* (The Experiment, 2021); Mark L. Clifford's *Today Hong Kong, Tomorrow the World* (St. Martin's, 2022); Karen Cheung's *The Impossible City: A Hong Kong Memoir* (Random House, 2022); Edmund W. Cheng and Samson Yuan's *The Making of Leaderful Contention: Power and Contention in Hong Kong* (Cambridge, 2024); Brian Kern's *Liberate Hong Kong:*

Stories from the Freedom Struggle (Bui Jones Books, 2024), originally published under the pseudonym Kong Tsung-gan; and Au Loong-Yu's *Hong Kong in Revolt* (Pluto, 2020).

Four books that engage with recent political events while offering valuable insights into earlier periods, two by journalists and two by social scientists, are particularly noteworthy. The two by journalists are Louisa Lim's *Indelible City: Dispossession and Defiance in Hong Kong* (Riverhead, 2022) and Shibani Mahtani and Timothy McLaughlin's *Among the Braves: Hope, Struggle, and Exile in the Battle for Hong Kong and the Future of Global Democracy* (Hachette, 2023). The social scientists' contributions are Ho-Fung Hung's *City on the Edge: Hong Kong Under Chinese Rule* (Cambridge, 2022) and Ching Kwan Lee's *Hong Kong: Global China's Restless Frontier* (Cambridge, 2022). Also worth special mention is *Aftershock: Essays from Hong Kong* (2020), a short volume of poignant reportage works edited by Holmes Chan.

Burma

For a basic background on Burma, covering ethnic divides and various strategies the military has used to maintain control, the following six books are valuable in different ways. Martin Smith's *Burma: Insurgents and the Politics of Ethnicity* (Zed, 1999) is a comprehensive 544-page volume that provides an authoritative account of the rise and fall of political parties and armed groups and the civil wars that began after independence and, in many cases, continue today. A useful work to supplement it on the recent past is Thant Myint-U's *The Hidden History of Burma: Race, Capitalism, and the Crisis of Democracy in the 21st Century* (Norton, 2021). On methods of control, Mary P. Callahan's *Making Enemies: War and State Building in*

Burma (Cornell, 2003) is particularly strong. Emma Larkin's *Finding George Orwell in Burma* (Penguin, 2006) offers a more impressionistic perspective, blending memoir and travel writing with historical insights. A compelling work of fiction is Charmaine Craig's *Miss Burma* (2017, Grove Atlantic), in which the author tenderly shares how her family participated in and endured Burma's tumultuous twentieth century. Lastly, Clare Hammond's *On the Shadow Tracks: A Journey through Occupied Myanmar* (Allen Lane, 2024) is a recent debut by a journalist; based on trips across Burma before the coup, it reflects on the coup and its aftermath.

For an introduction to youth activism, Win Min's chapter in the Aspinall and Weiss volume is an excellent starting point. Aung Tun's *A History of the Burmese Student Movement* (The Union Publishing, 2007) is also valuable. For insights specifically on the 1988 protests, see Bertil Lintner's *Outrage: Burma's Struggle for Democracy*, second edition (Weatherhill, 1995). (Note: Lintner's new book, *The Golden Land Ablaze: Coups, Insurgents and the State in Myanmar*, just released by Hurst Books, focuses on recent events and would have been included here if it had come out a few months earlier.) On the Saffron Revolution, see Rosalind Russell's *Burma's Spring: Real Lives in Turbulent Times* (River Books, 2015) and Human Rights Watch's *Crackdown: Repression of the 2007 Popular Protests in Burma* (Human Rights Watch, 2007). Emma Larkin's *Everything is Broken: A Tale of Catastrophe in Burma* (Penguin, 2010) also covers the 2007 protests but centers on the aftermath of Cyclone Nargis in 2008, highlighting the government's tragic mishandling of this natural disaster.

Several works by ethnographers offer valuable insights into various aspects of Burmese developments over the past decade or so. Two of the most notable are Ardeth Thawnghmung's *Everyday Economic Survival in Myanmar* (University of Wisconsin Press, 2019) and Elliott Prasse-Freeman's *Rights Refused: Grassroots Activism and State Violence in Myanmar* (Stanford, 2023), which focuses on strategies of resistance and is particularly relevant to the themes of this book.

For insight into the Rohingya genocide, I recommend the following resources beyond traditional books. On the former topic, the Crisis Group has published a series of detailed reports, accessible through the Myanmar section of its website: https://www.crisisgroup.org/asia/south-east-asia/myanmar. For an academic perspective on the rhetoric that laid the groundwork for the violence, see the article by Nickey Diamond and Ken MacLean, "Dangerous Speech Cloaked in Saffron Robes: Race, Religion, and Anti-Muslim Violence in Myanmar," in *The Routledge Handbook of Religion, Mass Atrocity, and Genocide* (2021), pp. 205–216. Additionally, Matt Schissler's "Beyond Hate Speech and Misinformation: Facebook and the Rohingya Genocide in Myanmar" (*Journal of Genocide Research*, 2024, pp. 1–26) examines the role of social media in the crisis.

Regarding Aung San Suu Kyi, Timothy McLaughlin's profile in *The Atlantic*, "The Political Obituary of Aung San Suu Kyi" (December 7, 2021), succinctly outlines the dramatic shift in her reputation during the 2010s.

For insight into both the coup and the resistance to it, a good starting point is Ma Thida's *A-Maze: Myanmar's Struggle for Democracy, 2011–2023* (Balestier, 2024). Another accessible work, focusing on the military, is Oliver Slow's *Return of the Junta: Why Myanmar's Military Must Go Back to the Barracks* (Bloomsbury, 2023). For comprehensive and critical reporting on all aspects of the post-coup crisis, the online news magazine *Frontier Myanmar* provides regular long-form features available on its website without paywall: https://www.frontiermyanmar.net/en/.

Notable video reports include Soe Mao Aung, Ivan Ogilvie, Kyri Evangelou, and Charlie Philips's "On the Frontline of Myanmar's Coup Protests" (*The Guardian*, March 5, 2021), available at https://www.theguardian.com/world/video/2021/mar/05/on-the-frontline-of-myanmars-coup-protests-we-dont-accept-this-dictatorship-video; and Hannah Beech, Nikolay Nikolov, and Adam Ferguson's "A Trip to the Frontlines of a Forgotten War" (*The New York Times*, April 20, 2024), accessible at https://www.nytimes.com/video/world/asia/100000009411449/myanmar-democracy-fighters.html.

Finally, a fitting close is the anthology *Picking Off New Shoots Will Not Stop the Spring: Witness Poems and Essays from Burma/Myanmar (1988–2021)*, edited by Ko Ko Thett and Brian Haman (Ethos Books, 2022), which spans the resistance from 1988 to the time Nickey Diamond went into exile.

ACKNOWLEDGMENTS

This is a very short book, but by necessity one that needs a very long acknowledgments section. This is in part because work on *The Milk Tea Alliance* involved writing about and sometimes traveling to unfamiliar as well as familiar places. I accumulated large debts to both people who helped me see novel facets of settings and topics I thought I knew well, and even larger ones to people who proved patient guides to me in my efforts to understand places that I had never written about before and that they know so well. I depended more than in any past project on having friends and colleagues look over sections to make sure I had gotten things right, but all mistakes remaining are purely my responsibility.

I should begin by thanking three people I profiled who generously answered what must have seemed at times a stream of questions from me about their lives that would never end: Netiwit Chotiphatphaisal, Tun Myint, and Nickey Diamond. Several other activists in Bangkok and exiles from Hong Kong and Burma also graciously shared their experiences with me. Sometimes they only ended up getting a passing mention in this volume or were not referred to by name at all, even if their conversations with me informed points I made. In the case of some who are not mentioned, they may be glad of that and will not be named here. Some of the people I had exchanges with who I know are fine with being thanked are Krittapas, Mew, and Settanant (all members of what I think of as the Sam Yan Group); Nathan Law (who I met with in both London and California); Patrick Poon (who I met with twice in Tokyo); Alex Chow (who I met with in both DC and Taipei); Akkarasorn "Ang-Ang" Opilan (who met with me in London and who introduced me to an activist friend of hers); and Joey Siu (whose comments about traveling to Athens ahead of the 2022 Olympics with a Tibetan activist to call for a boycott of the second Beijing Games and "getting thrown into a foreign jail" together in a way bonded the two women in "special ways" and made them "best friends" for life I found very moving—even if I ended up being unable to find a natural way to include them in the main text and so am sneaking them in here).

I also owe special debts of gratitude to two people who provided research assistance and editorial advice rooted in area expertise. One of these was my collaborator on this book, who is identified here, at his request, by the pseudonym Prad Sirisomboon. Through a stroke of very good luck, Prad, who was an eyewitness to many 2020 protests, was one of the first people I met in Bangkok. He remains one of the most interesting Thai youths I have encountered—and that is saying a lot because several of the activists I met (he is not an activist) are extraordinary people. Prad worked with me for more than a year on the general ideas in the book and my handling of Bangkok events, while also providing language for some short sections of exposition and translating materials. I was able, late in the process, to begin working with a graduate student in Burmese studies (who would prefer to remain anonymous); this student assisted me very ably on the penultimate chapter in some of the ways that Prad had on earlier ones.

In addition to the activists who I profiled and Prad, I owe special thanks to three people from Milk Tea Alliance settings. One is Wichuta Teeratanobodee, who I have somehow still never encountered in real life, but I have learned a lot from via our Zoom conversations and email exchanges and through co-authorship of two articles. A second is Jeffrey Ngo, a Hong Kong exile of the Milk Tea Alliance generation, a talented early-stage Hong Kong historian, and someone whose past experience as part of the same circle as Agnes Chow helped make up for my being unable to interview her for this book. The third is Francis (full name: Bunkueanun Paothong), who may only make a brief appearance in the book, but whose willingness to spend time talking with me and showing me around in Bangkok on two different occasions was crucial in the creation of the Thailand chapter.

I owe additional debts to many other people who met with me in Bangkok, talked to me about Thai history and politics, and otherwise helped me understand things about Netiwit and his world. My visits to Bangkok were greatly enriched by encounters with Gwen Robinson, Emma Larkin, Panu Wongcha-um, and Wasana Wongsurawat, as well as by a short but intense conversation there with Tyrell Haberkorn. Exchanges with Tyrell on Thailand in other parts of the world over the course of years have also benefited me enormously, and the same is true for my interactions with three other leading scholars of the country: Duncan McCargo, Thongchai Winichakul, and Claudio Sopranzetti. Meetings to discuss Thailand or online exchanges about it with the following people while I was working on this book also meant a lot to me: Tomas Larsson, Penchan Phoborisut, Pongkwan Sawasdipakdi, Tuwonont Phattharathanasut, and James Buchanan. A special thanks is due to Kanokrat Lertchoosakul, for her insights and her patience with someone stumbling into terrain she has mapped with exquisite care for a long time was extraordinary. I also was pleased to be able to meet with and get feedback on my project from two Thai exiles of pre-Milk Tea Alliance generations who I met up with in Europe in one case and Asia in the other: Jaran Ditapichai (long based in Paris) and Pavin Chachavalpongpun (long based in Kyoto). And though I did not manage to meet up in Bangkok with Hannah Beech—who has done impressive reporting on Hong Kong, Thailand, and Burma—she added a lot to what I got out of my visits to that city simply by connecting me to Gwen, who connected me to Francis and Panu and many of the other people thanked above and hosted the first public talk on this project I gave in Southeast Asia.

Regarding Hong Kong, an extensive list of people I have learned important things about the city from over the years can be found in the acknowledgments section of *Vigil*. While working specifically on this book, I have had valuable conversations and/or online exchanges with the following people: Sharon Yam, Jessie Lau, Amy Hawkins, Denise Y. Ho, C. K. Lee, Gina Tam, Mark Frazier, Sebastian Veg, Edmund Cheng, James Carter, Deborah Davis, Tammy Ho, Shibani Mahtani, Tim McLaughlin, Elaine Yu, Mary Hui, Ilaria Maria Sala, and Evan Fowler.

Regarding Burma, people who have shared their knowledge with me, either many times over the years or in a specific meeting while I was working on this book, include Ma Thida, Matt Schissler, and Thant Myint-U. My Thailand-based friend Emma Larkin deserves a second thank you here, and I am grateful that both she and Elliott Prasse-Freeman, another author of important works on Burma, made time to read and comment on complete drafts.

On transnational activism, I benefited, sometimes in ways they may not even be aware of, from conversations with: Heonik

Kwon, Julia Lovell, Jordan Sand, Rachel Leow, Jeff Kingston, Gregory B. Lee, Odd Arne Westad, Yangyang Cheng, Tessa Wong, Meredith Weiss, Micah Alpaugh, Miklós Haraszti, Isabel Hilton, Neal Ascherson, Misha Glenny, Pankaj Mishra, Padraic Kenney, Valerie Bunce, Tom Pepinsky, Timothy Garton Ash, Howard French, Adam Hochschild, Ian Johnson, Natalya Chernyshova, Eraldo Souza dos Santos, Stephen Sawyer, Diu-Huong Nguyen, Ian Rowen, Lev Nachman, Brian Hioe, Manan Ahmed, Peter Frankopan, Amy Wilentz, Emily Baum, Brian Spivey, Lien-Hang Nguyen, David Kaye, Josh Freeman, Perry Anderson, Grace Tsoi, Wang Chaohua, Lee Haiyan, Elizabeth Perry, Zoher Abdoolcarim, Feliz Solomon, Julia McCarthy, James Robson, Amanda Imasaka, Umemori Naoyuki, Ben Nathans, Ed Pulford, and Rian Thum.

I am grateful to many friends and family members as well—all the ones I have mentioned in the acknowledgments to my previous books and some new ones, too—who supported my move in this new direction in various ways. In some cases, they gave me things to smile about even when the news from the places that I was focusing on was depressing, and they all put up with hearing report after report about where I was going and what I was finding out. I also want to thank the institutions that hosted me when I was trying out ideas for this book, as well as the audience members and especially the moderators and commentators at those events. Thanks are due to the University of Vienna, the American University in Paris, the University of Edinburgh, Yale, Harvard, Columbia, Cambridge, the Institute for Advanced Study in Princeton, Pomona College, the National Taiwan Normal University, Birkbeck College (University of London), and Warwick University. Special shout outs are also due to the in-person salon that David Bandurski convened in

Taipei; the Zoom-based "Asia Beyond Borders" occasional seminar whose members gave me valuable comments on a proposed opening for the book; and Choon Hwee Koh and Minh Bui Jones, who read and gave me useful comments on early drafts (and on a later one, too, in the latter case).

I feel very fortunate to have once again gotten the chance to see my prose improved by Jimmy So's edits and be able to work a second time with other members of the Columbia Global Reports team. Special thanks there to Nicholas Lemann, for having the faith in my ability to do something largely not about the places I had spent most of my career working on, and to Camille McDuffie, for her support right up to the day she retired.

I want to end by thanking Birkbeck College, a very special institution that has been ravaged by bruising cuts. I am glad to be based at UC Irvine and have the support I get from colleagues in its History Department and other units, especially the Forum for the Academy and the Public that I co-direct with Amy Wilentz. Key parts of this book, though, were written in 2023 in an office that Birkbeck College provided me with while, thanks to the hard work of Julia Lovell, I spent three months there as a Leverhulme Visiting Professor (my thanks to the Leverhulme Trust as well). The award gave me a chance to meet some of Julia's extraordinary colleagues and students and try out ideas for this book in the last of a series of four public lectures I gave. The office I wrote in was at the edge of Russell Square, which is home to an outdoor café that served as an ideal place to meet up with Milk Tea Alliance members, both temporary sojourners in London and exiles. Out the window I had a view of SOAS, a hub for study of both East and Southeast Asia. Birkbeck was founded with a commitment to progressive goals and it has a

History Department that was long the home to the author of the first book I read that placed uprisings in different parts of the world side by side: Eric Hobsbawm's *Primitive Rebels*. From my base there I was able to take walks and bus rides to sites such as the place Sun Yat-sen was kidnapped while a political exile and Trafalgar Square, which I went to on June 4 to attend a vigil attended by more than a few people who, like me, had been to the last legal Tiananmen commemoration held in Hong Kong. Birkbeck was, in short, the perfect place to be based while grappling with the ideas explored and thinking about the special people profiled in this book.

NOTES

INTRODUCTION

oo **Edward Beauchamp:** Edward R. Beauchamp, review of *Students in Revolt*, in *Journal of Higher Education*, May 1970, pp. 414–416.

oo **with some former student leaders gaining seats as MPs:** Kanokrat Lertchoosokul, "The May 2023 Elections and the Triumph of Thai Youth Social Movements," *Critical Asian Studies*, May 30, 2023.

oo **thwarting the popular will and dissolved the party:** The events in Thailand last year were not only a reprise of earlier moves there but fit in with trends across the regions, as Joshua Kurlantzick notes in "The State of Democracy in Southeast Asia is Bad and Getting Worse," *World Politics Review*, August 9, 2023.

oo **translated into Burmese, so that it could be read by anti-coup activists:** Mary Hui, "Hong Kongers Crowdsourced a Protest Manual—And Myanmar's Already Using It," *Quartz*, February 25, 2021.

oo **sense of connection across geographical, cultural, and linguistic divides, often referred to as the "Milk Tea Alliance":** The BBC interview was posted on November 8, 2020, the Reuters article on February 28, 2021.

PART ONE

oo **the Thai Education Revolution Alliance:** The 2012 group is mentioned in, among other places, this recent news article on Netiwit that has a good precis of his activism career up to the present: Thai PBS World Political Desk, "Democracy to Heritage: Activist Netiwit Hailed for 'Last Breath of Sam Yan,'" *Thai PBS World*, October 3, 2024.

oo **called Thaksin a "crook" and a "dictator in the guise of democracy":** Transcript from a September 17, 2010, segment of *Democracy Now* titled "Large Anti-Government Protests Scheduled on Fourth Anniversary of the Coup."

oo **wants to see the representatives of the current structure live up to their own ideals:** Sulak Sivaraksa, *Loyalty Demands Dissents: Autobiography of an Engaged Buddhist* (Parallax, 1998).

oo **they became fast friends:** My reconstruction of this series of events is based mainly on my exchanges with Netiwit in English and an interview that my collaborator Prad Sirisomboon conducted with him in Thai. I also draw on Tuwanot Phattaranthanusat, "From Bad Student to Transnational Activist: Netiwit Chotiphatphaisal and Transnational Activism in Northeast and Southeast Asia,"

Trans: Transregional and National Studies of Southeast Asia, January 19, 2024, which includes the photographs Netiwit took with Joshua Wong and Nathan Law on the day of their first meeting. This part of the chapter and others as well also benefit greatly from information shared with me by Panu Wongcha-um, a veteran Bangkok-based reporter who has covers Thai politics insightfully and carefully for *Reuters* for years; and Wichuta Teeratanabodee. Both have interviewed Netiwit at length in Thai. For the Hong Kong side of the events of October 2016, I benefited from discussions with Jeffrey Ngo.

oo **had abolished prostration:** Asaree Thaitrakulpanich, "Thorn in the Pillar: Freshman Makes Enemies Upsetting Tradition. Allies Too," *Khaosoden English*, September 25, 2016.

oo **"dismissals from the student council were less about misconduct than undermining what Netiwit represents":** Patpicha Tanakasempipat, "Thai University Removes Student Leader for Defying Royalist Tradition," *Reuters*, September 1, 2017.

oo **his status as the leader of the protest soon became clear:** Teeranai Charuvastra, "Initiation Walkout Costs Netiwit Student Presidency," *Khaosoden English*, August 31, 2018.

oo **"rare critic of the military junta":** Patpicha Tanakasempipat, "Thai University Removes Student Leader for Defying Royalist Tradition," *Reuters*, September 1, 2017.

oo **as if a baton had been passed from Hong Kong to Bangkok:** I later saw the relay race invoked in a similar way in a work Timothy Garton Ash was writing at the same time, *Homelands: A Personal History of Europe* (Yale, 2023).

oo **uses the term "protest swapping":** For Buchanan's use of the phrase, see Mary Hui, "Thailand and Hong Kong Protesters Are Brewing a Strong #MilkTeaAlliance," *Quartz*, October 19, 2020.

PART TWO

oo **"send a warning to anyone who dares to openly criticize the government that they could be next":** Amnesty International, "Hong Kong: Jailed Opposition Activists Must be Released," press release, December 2, 2020.

PART THREE

oo **"I saw the shooting in front of me":** "Carleton College Professor Draws from His Own Past to Teach Students about Burma Conflict," *MPR News*, October 18, 2007.

oo **"minority ethnic people interpreted the erection of the**

102 **statue as part of Burmanisation":** Victoria Milko, "Ethnic Minorities across Myanmar Protest against Aung San Statues," *Al Jazeera*, March 29, 2019. There are differing perspectives on the statue's meaning and the surrounding dispute. Karenni nationalists take pride in the British recognition of their territory as sovereign, even while other areas of present-day Burma were under colonial rule. For them, Aung San would *not* have been a revered figure.

CONCLUSION

00 **early twentieth-century activists profiled by Tim Harper:** Tim Harper, *Underground Asia: Global Revolutionaries and the Assault on Empire*, Allen Lane, 2019.

Columbia Global Reports is a nonprofit publishing imprint from Columbia University that commissions authors to produce works of original thinking and on-site reporting from all over the world, on a wide range of topics. Our books are short—novella-length, and readable in a few hours—but ambitious. They offer new ways of looking at and understanding the major issues of our time. Most readers are curious and busy. Our books are for them.

If this book changed the way you look at the world, and if you would like to support our mission, consider making a gift to Columbia Global Reports to help us share new ideas and stories.

Visit globalreports.columbia.edu to support our upcoming books, subscribe to our newsletter, and learn more about Columbia Global Reports. Thank you for being part of our community of readers and supporters.

The Lie Detectives: In Search of a Playbook for Winning Elections in the Disinformation Age
Sasha Issenberg

Soul by Soul: The Evangelical Mission to Spread the Gospel to Muslims
Adriana Carranca

In Defense of Partisanship
Julian Zelizer

Climate Radicals: Why Our Environmental Politics Isn't Working
Cameron Abadi

Left Adrift: What Happened to Liberal Politics
Timothy Shenk

Losing Big: America's Reckless Bet on Sports Gambling
Jonathan D. Cohen